Dorothy Paull (author)

SCARLET FEVER

A story of early years in Banff and my life
as a Royal Canadian Mounted Policeman's wife.

1914 - 1956

DOROTHY STANDISH PAULL

LAURAL CHVOJKA, EDITOR

Published in Canada

Copyright © 1993
Dorothy Standish Paull
and Laural Chvojka

All rights reserved. No part of this book may be reproduced in any form or by any electronic or mechanical means including information storage and retrieval systems without permission in writing from the publisher, except by a reviewer, who may quote brief passages in a review.

For More Information Contact:
   Dorothy Paull, Publisher   Betty Fraser
   #302 - 1520 Vidal St.   R.R. 2
   White Rock, B.C.   Lacombe, Alberta
   V4B 3T7   T0C 1S0

ISBN 0-9697242-0-9

Printed May, 1993
Adviser Graphics, Red Deer, Alberta

I dedicate this book to my husband Tommy, our family and friends who have enriched my life and have given me the memories that have inspired me to write Scarlet Fever.

Laural Chvojka, editor and Dorothy Paull author, when family memories turned into Alberta History and were developed into the book Scarlet Fever.

I would like to thank the Whyte Museum in Banff and our niece Gayle Darby for their assistance in providing some of the photographs for this book.
Dorothy Paull

iii

Author's Notes March 1993

Writing these memories have brought back many thoughts of my early years in Banff. My life has been guided by so many family and friends. Our grandmother, who gave up her retirement years to care for and mould the lives of her two motherless grandchildren. She gave us the foundation to live a good Christian life.

Our Grandfather was a jolly, kind person with a great love and respect for his fellowman. No person was ever turned away hungry from our home during the depression years. Grandpa had a great way with animals - I think he had a kindred spirit. There was a buck deer with a great expanse of antlers that come to the back door quite regularly. Grandpa was small in stature, but he'd twist those great antlers and guide the animal into the kitchen to eat an apple off of the kitchen table. After the treat he would again twist the antlers and back him out the door. Fortunately nothing ever happened to alarm the animal and I hate to think what might have happened if it had.

Grandpa and Grandma were generous people. Each fall a hundred gallons of maple syrup would arrive from the maple syrup farm in Rougemont Quebec, that they had left to come west. Our grandparents gave most of the syrup away to Banff neighbours and friends. The first fall of snow was the occasion for a great treat for my brother and I. While we went out to fill the wash tub with new clean fresh snow Grandpa boiled up the maple syrup to spread over the snow for maple crackle-how good that was.

Memories of our Mother are few as she was spared to be with us for such a short time. Her passing was a great loss to us all but especially to our Father and the many friends she had made in her short time in Banff. I have felt her closeness many times during my lifetime.

Our father taught us so many things — to be a good sport and to be a good loser. I came in near the end of many races but as long as I came in smiling he was proud of me. Our father had many heartaches in life but was well thought of. He was a kind amiable man and enjoyed showing visitors around his beloved mountain town. He taught me the appreciation of the opportunity we had to live in this beautiful area. My father passed away in 1959 and all the family are buried in the Standish plot in the Banff Cemetery for oldtimers.

Now in 1993 a recent trip to Banff with Laural our editor, daughters Betty and Connie was a special treat. We went in the spring of 1993 before the book was published and brought back many memories.

We stood on the bank of the frozen river where Mrs. Gratz watched me every morning when I was canoeing.

Crossing the bridge, Laural took pictures of the Indian heads on the river side of the bridge. She took pictures of the Green Spot, now white and Mount Norquay where we could see the ski runs.

Snow was blowing off the picturesque Mount Rundle Mountain, indicating a chinook (warming trend) was on the way.

The majestic Cascade mountain was loaded with snow that day.

We drove to the Cave and Basin, where we entered the cave to view the pool used in earlier days by the Indians.

We passed the headquarters that used to house the fish hatchery, on our way to the Bow Falls. The Falls are still beautiful in its winter frozen appearance.

We had lots of laughs as I realized our daughters had always thought, and had told their friends that their mother had canoed down over the Bow Falls. Not only once but many times. It was the Bow Rapids instead not the Bow Falls that I had canoed down. The Bow Rapids are located between Banff and Castle Mountain.

Finally the view of Tunnel Mountain as we passed where our house on 110 Beaver Street used to be. Before leaving town we drove past Canmore to photograph the "Three Sisters" as we left my former mountain home.

Mount Rundle with chinook wind blowing the snow

Banff with Cascade mountain in the background

Taken in Banff Alberta, February 1993. Left to right. Daughter Betty, Dorothy Paull, daughter Connie, and Laural editor, in front of ice palace.

Dorothy, Betty and Connie by the frozen Bow Falls

Tunnel Mountain

Three Sisters at Canmore after we left Banff on our way home

TABLE OF CONTENTS

CHAPTER I - B.C. BEGINNINGS 1

CHAPTER II - BANFF CELEBRATIONS 15

CHAPTER III - BANFF SIGHTS 25

CHAPTER IV - CATCHING SCARLET FEVER 37

CHAPTER V - CONSTABLE TOM PAULL 41

CHAPTER VI - OUR FIRST POSTING - MAGRATH 49

CHAPTER VII - TRANSFERRED TO LETHBRIDGE 53

CHAPTER VIII - NORTHERN POSTING - FORT MCMURRAY . . . 55

CHAPTER IX - LEARNING TO COPE 77

CHAPTER X - OUR NORTHERN YEARS END - NEW POSTING
   - STETTLER 95

CHAPTER XI - SICKNESS HITS OUR LITTLE GIRL 99

CHAPTER XII - OUR NEXT MOVE - OLDS, ALBERTA 103

CHAPTER XIII - SOUTH TO HIGH RIVER 109

CHAPTER XIV - LIVING IN HARMONY 113

CHAPTER XV - RETIREMENT 117

B.C. BEGINNINGS

Around the year 1886 my grandparents, Sias and Tilly Standish and my father, Gordon, came west from Rougemont, Quebec to start their pioneer lives. Property was bought in Burnaby, British Columbia and a ninety-nine year lease was signed in Banff, Alberta. They established businesses in both of the towns.

In January 1912 my father brought his bride, Louise Watkins, from Toronto and they started their home in Burnaby, on the corner of Douglas Road and Edmond Street; now Edmond Street and Canada Way. They built a commercial block which included a grocery store, and several other stores with living quarters on the second floor. The grocery store was named the "Mayflower Cash Grocery" after the ship on which Miles Standish, an early pioneer arrived from England.

Sias, Tilly and Gordon Standish

My grandparents continued to build up the lumber and hardware business in Banff. My brother Austin and I were both born in the Royal Columbia hospital in New Westminster.

While my brother and I were still very young, my parents moved to Banff and built two homes on Beaver Street. My grandparents decided to return to a milder climate. They traded places with us and took over the business at the coast.

A flu epidemic struck our home in 1918 leaving my brother and me motherless, so my grandparents moved back to Banff to care for us. My grandparents and father worked together in the hardware business.

Mother (formally Louise Watkins) and Dad (Gordon), Dorothy and Austin – Christmas 1914

The first hardware store consisted of a two storey white building with a Masonic hall on the top floor. The boiler in the basement blew up one winter day and fire gutted the store. Since the store was insured, we had it rebuilt with three rental suites upstairs and an electrical room in the store. A short in the electrical room caused another fire and gutted the upstairs front suites. The back suite was saved and this was the one that I later moved into. Once again we had the store rebuilt, putting in a fire proof ceiling. The store remained like this until government regulations required Banff businesses to be built out of Rundle rock. The old white store was moved and remains as a dormitory for one of the hotels.

Grandpa Standish (Sias) in front of our home on 110 BeaverStreet

Dorothy and Austin Standish, 1918

Recent and last picture of Banff home with Anglican Church in the background, 1990

Indian days parade with the Standish store in the background, 1926

Standish block, before store built of Rundle rock

Tillie and Sias Standish, 1920

The new store was majestic and covered an entire block. It housed a service station, the hardware store, a dental office, a coin laundry, and a bakery. It looked indestructible.

However, early one morning, a fire started in the coin laundry going through the floor. It was thought that the fire was started by a gas leak. Again on Dec. 7, 1960 fire gutted the store. Once more the store was rebuilt, this time managed by my brother. Having the store destroyed by fire so often was almost too much for the family to bear. Following my brother's death, his family carried on the business.

The Standish Hardware is still in the same place. It has changed in appearance several times due to fires and government regulations. The hardware is still run by the fourth generation of the Standish family. (Note: in 1991 the store was torn down and a modern shopping centre put in its place. There is a plaque set in the spot where the store stood.)

Standish block with new stores

My brother passed away at the young age of 52 — a great loss for me as we just had each other most of our youth. The relationship I had with my brother was very unique and special. Austin showed me a loving concern that few siblings ever share.

My brother and I were close in age and grew up to be great pals, however, there were times, I am sure I was a nuisance to him. Our grandmother insisted that on Saturdays, Austin had to look after his little sister. This was the day that the boys on one side of town would challenge the boys on the other side of town to games of cops and robbers on Tunnel Mountain. Austin would take me along but when we got near to where they were playing he would tie me to a tree. This was to make sure I would not run away and get lost, but he would leave me something with which to amuse myself. After the game I would trot happily home, having enjoyed the outing of being with my brother.

Dorothy and Austin Standish, 1930

Austin and Dorothy (I'm wearing the coat that Austin gave me as a Christmas gift

When he was older and worked as a bus driver for Rocky Mountain Tour Lines he always shared his tip money with me. He always remembered my birthday, by buying me something special like a new dress, something I would never have been able to afford myself. My memories of my brother are very warm and a rich treasure of love for me.

This is how our lives started in the beautiful town of Banff located in the Canadian Rockies. I have many memories of growing up in this place of natural beauty and it still fills me with nostalgia.

Green spot on the mountain in the winter

It is interesting to recall the wonders of nature that I enjoyed in Banff. On the way up to Mount Norquay there is a large area called the Green Spot, a place where no trees grow. I do not know why trees do not grow in this large area. There are many legends that it was an Indian "Hallowed area." As far back as I can remember it was and is the same, the Green Spot on the mountain.

In the earlier years before the road went up to the ski area, the Green Spot was a wonderful place to hike too. It was a neat place to have a picnic and enjoy the view of the town of Banff. In the spring a variety of flowers grew on this treeless spot. There were crocuses, forget-me-nots, shooting stars, buttercups, lady slippers, and many other beautiful blooms.

I can't remember the year but it was sometime in the 1920's, when our father, my brother, I, and many other adults climbed Mount Cory to the "Hole in the Wall." This was a large cave in the mountain between Banff and Johnson Canyon. It was a challenging climb but well worth it to stand in the entrance of that massive cavern. The mouth of the cavern looked to be about forty-five feet across and thirty feet high. I had my picture taken in the mouth of the cave and I looked like a midget in comparison. (Unfortunately, the pictures were in the store when we had the fire, so I am unable to show any here. Along with the pictures, we also lost many of the trophies and medals won by my father and my brother in various sports competitions.) We didn't go into the cave because we could tell by the droppings outside, that it was a shelter for wild mountain animals. The view from the cave was breath taking as we sat and ate our lunch, over looking the valley below.

Maybe that was the beginning of my brother Austin's desire to climb. This he did with his friends, scaling most of the mountains around Banff and area during his teenage years.

During our early years in Banff it was with great anticipation that we looked forward to the visit from our Akhurst relatives. They would come to see us during the summer holidays. Aunt Tillie Akhurst was the niece of our grandmother and possibly named after her. Uncle Ed was a builder and earlier built many of the buildings in Bankhead and in Banff. We loved to hear the interesting stories of the unsinkable S.S. Titanic's going down after it hit an iceberg. Uncle Ed, Aunt Tillie and infant daughter May escaped sailing from England on this ship. There was no more room on the S.S. Titanic, so they came safely to Canada on another ship.

They used to come and pitch their tent in the yard. Sometimes they would stay in the cottage behind the house, called "the Outside Inn" or join the family in our house. Their children May, Monty, and Carden were like family to my brother and me. What fun we had and what treats we enjoyed as Uncle Ed spoiled us with goodies! I will always remember those summers and the joy of their special place in our lives.

We fed the deer with our apple peels at the back door. Occasionally, my grandfather coaxed them in, to nibble their treats off of the kitchen table. Black bears roamed and usually had the contents of our garbage pails well scattered as they looked for choice morsels on which to dine. We didn't feel fear as we went around town among those animals. The bears just went about their business in their home, the National Park.

During my years of growing up in Banff, I was cautious of the animals. I never did hear of a real tragedy caused by the animals in the park. The deer roamed in large numbers and were beautiful but timid creatures. Usually in the fall the elk entered the town area. Then we seldom saw deer, as these much larger animals took over the territory. The elk were not the friendly animal everyone believed them to be. We learned at an early age to be cautious when they were around.

Elk near Banff

Only once do I recall a near tragic accident with an elk. One of the huge bucks with an expanse of horns caught a little fellow up in his antlers. The youngster was hung up by the braces of his overalls. The lad, may have teased the elk. When the elk threw back his head, the braces of the little fellow's overalls broke. Fortunately, the lad was thrown at the base of a tree in the bush, where the animal was unable to reach him. The game warden arrived on the scene, and the elk who may have been a danger to others lost his life. The little boy was unharmed other then having a few scratches and being a little shaken. This was a reminder to any of us who might have felt that these animals were friendly. We were all shocked into remembering the elk were wild animals and not as gentle as the deer we always welcomed back to wander about the town.

Another animal that also entered the town was the cougar. I remember on one occasion when we were told to stay in the classroom after school, until a game warden captured and removed the cougar roaming on the school grounds.

Another occasion stands out vividly in my mind of our relationship with the mountain animal dwellers. Before modern skiers and before roads up to the now famous Norquay Ski resort, early skiers would ski to the foot of the mountain which was about a mile from Banff, and would climb the trail used as a log shoot. At the top we would find the small ski lodge, nestled at the foot of this excellent skiing area. Often on Saturday afternoons, several of us would go there for an afternoon ski. After our supper we would have a moonlight ski down the log trail and then the cross country trip home.

One time I worked late at the dental office and was unable to leave when my companions did. It was later in the afternoon when I took off alone. By the time I reached the logging trail the early dark of winter was upon me. The moon was not yet up to shed its light on the path. I climbed the trail in the semi-darkness. Somewhere in the long shadows cast by the tall trees I could hear the occasional snap of a twig. Although I couldn't see anything, I had the uncanny feeling that I had company as I travelled the lonesome trail. I felt great fear as I neared the top of the climb. Within sight of the cabin, I strapped on my skis. I made those last few yards in record time. I related my fears to my companions, one of whom was a game warden, and when he made a check around, sure enough my unseen guest had been a cougar. His tracks were as fresh as my own, and they lead right up to the cabin door. Fortunately for me, I was above the stalking cougar. Maybe he was just curious and enjoyed my company on the evening climb. My companions and I returned to Banff safely that evening without any harm done to any of us.

One interesting place that I remember I liked to visit regularly during my early days in Banff, was the Banff Zoo. This was located behind the red brick picturesque R.C.M.P. building, a choice location along the banks of the Bow River. There were many animals housed there, from "Buddy" the Polar Bear to the ground hog. Many watched each spring to see if the ground hog came out and saw his shadow which is a sign to show if winter was over or would stay around a bit longer.

At the four o'clock feeding time it was so interesting to see the enthusiasm of the animals getting their food. "Buddy" used to dive into his pool to catch the fish that were thrown to him. Also, there were a large variety of birds, including a talking crow. Sometimes he would chatter away and say "hello," but often he would be stubborn and not say a word until we left. As soon as we were out of sight he would either say "good-bye" or give a hearty laugh. As I remember he also had a few choice words some people preferred he didn't use. He was very interesting and fun to watch. I spent many a happy hour watching the animals.

The area around the zoo was a wonderful place to have a picnic among the poplar trees. Especially in the fall of the year with the poplar trees in all their variety of colours. When the many poplar trees around the zoo lost their leaves early in the fall, I especially loved to walk through the leaves ankle deep before the snow fell. I think maybe the reason I enjoy walking through fall leaves even now is that it brings back wonderful memories. It was a very sad time for me when the zoo closed and they moved the animals to various locations.

Many childhood memories pass through my mind of the 1920's. One that I think of often is about the tall gentleman, Mr. Samson. He made several trips every week up Sulphur Mountain to read the weather meter at the observation tower. This information was in turn passed on to the broadcasting system. He passed by our house equipped with his mountain gear. He reminded me of a giant when he took those four foot strides. Mr. Norman B. Samson had completed 1000 climbs to check equipment and change record blanks at the Observation station by 1931. I attended a celebration in recognition of Mr. Samson, on top of Sulphur Mountain where coffee was served to blanket covered climbers as we sat in a rainbow fairyland. The sun rose flooding the mountain top with many colours reflecting through the snow, falling gently on the valley and town of Banff below.

I recall the thrill of climbing Tunnel Mountain looking for the first crocus of spring. I would find it either poking its head through a crack in the rock or sometimes through the snow.

Wooden bridge over the Bow River with Cascade mountain in the background. Summer

New bridge over the Bow River, Cascade mountain in the background.

Memories of the wooden bridge that crossed the Bow River, brings many images to mind. I will never forget the sign at both ends of the bridge that read, "Walk your horses at both ends." Horses were still much in use during my young years although cars were beginning to appear.

In 1932, a massive new bridge replaced the old wooden bridge above the Bow River. Like most of the new buildings in Banff the sides of the bridge were built of Mt. Rundle Rock. On the outside facing the river were beautiful carvings of Indian heads, light standards were placed above each one. Unfortunately, the Indian heads which I thought were so majestic could only be seen from the ground after crossing the river. It's a shame more people don't know to look back to enjoy them.

Indian heads on the bridge

Banff had a street cleaner fondly called Dad Barnett. Mr. Barnett could be seen each day dressed in his white coat. He pushed a little cart where he put the street litter in that he had collected. There is a story told about a tourist who met Dad Barnett early one morning. The tourist asked him what there was to do in that one horse town. Mr. Barnett's reply was simple and to the point, "You would not think that it was a one horse town if you had my job!"

Once a week a garbage dray came up our lane to pick up the garbage. The gentleman Fred Day who performed this duty was an Oxford graduate. I learned a very important lesson from this cheerful and very friendly gentleman. "It is not what you do that counts but how you do it and the pleasures you find in your work." He must have really enjoyed life as I never recall seeing him unhappy.

Another memory was the daily delivery of quarts of milk at ten cents a quart. During the summer, as soon as the milkman delivered the milk, it was brought in quickly. It would be placed in the coolness of the basement to keep it from going sour. During the winter, although it was brought in quickly, it usually had a couple of inches of frozen cream on the top. The cardboard lid would sit loosely on the top of the frozen cream. Letting the milk sit at room temperature soon liquified it enough to make it useable. It didn't matter if it was a cold miserable day or a very hot day, the milkman always arrived six days a week.

Weekends in Banff and the booming towns around were especially lively in the early 1920's. One such town was Bankhead, a thriving coal mining town only a few miles from Banff on the way to Lake Minnewanka. Several hundred people lived and worked in Bankhead, famous for the fine coal and briquettes they mined and produced. On weekends and especially on Saturday night the town of Banff doubled in population. Residents of both towns gathered there to visit and party. I used to like to go with my grandparents in their Model T and park on main street. It was interesting to sit and watch the people.

The closing of Bankhead in 1922 was due to the high cost of production and the competition from other mines. This made a difference in Banff — not only on weekends. Many of the lovely miners homes were moved to Banff. Now with the buildings gone the town of Bankhead is just a ghost town. The last time I was there it was hard to find the location of the town. The foundations of the homes overgrown with foliage was all that remained of Bankhead. The memory of those happy days is something I treasure.

Another town remembered by my grandparents was Silver City, nestled under the tower of Castle Mountain. (Later named Mount Eisenhower and then later changed back to Castle Mountain.) In August 1881 an ore thought to be silver was discovered. It was really copper with only a small amount of silver content.

A few years later log houses, a hotel, and stores sprang up. This town soon became known as Silver city. This booming city soon had a population of 3000 people. It supported four stores, a post office, pool room, bakery, blacksmith shop, lime kiln, and brickyard as well as several restaurants.

Between the years of 1886 and 1888 much of the town was torn down. They shipped the logs to many places and used them to build C.P.R section houses. Even some of the early Banff hotels were built out of these logs.

The only resident who stayed was Joe Smith. He was the first to arrive there and the last person to leave. He spent his remaining years, trapping, hunting, and prospecting until he was nearly blind. He was taken to the Lacombe home at the age of 94, and he died in 1937.

I remember walking with my father among the decayed vegetation that covered the remains of log buildings as we tried to picture the former city.

One trip that we looked forward to, but only made occasionally was the trip to Field, British Columbia. In the early 1920's, it was a trip that would take a whole day to complete. The roads were narrow, rough, and usually only a one way traffic. The driver drove with one hand on the steering wheel and the other hand on the horn. In those days there were many signs that read, "Blow your horn" as you drove those twisty roads.

The road took us past Lake Louise and over the switch back road. What a feat to engineer the spiral tunnels which enabled the trains to move in a figure eight from lower elevation to higher elevation. What a thrill it was when we happened to arrive at the same time as the train. This was something to see, the old steam engines puffing along. Often there were two engines in front and two at the end of the train pushing their heavy loads. The rumble seemed to shake the mountains and possibly did so as it was an area of many snow and gravel slides.

It was on to Field, B.C., a small town of maybe a hundred people located at the base of Mount Stephen. Field was the headquarters for the Yoho National Park offices. The hub of Field was the old Mount Stephen Hotel, later taken over by the Y.M.C.A. It housed the railway station, the library, barber shop, dance hall, and the occasional theatre shows. Also found here were the offices for doctors and dentists when they made their monthly trip to that area. It had a fine restaurant with great food. I recall, that we could enjoy a full course steak dinner for a $1.00. In later years after the Y.M.C.A. was gone and with the new paved roads, I am glad to have those memories.

I remember trips with my father who hauled loads of lumber to the Lake Louise Station where the lumber was loaded onto tram cars and taken to be used to build the Lake Louise Hotel. These were exciting outings for a young girl.

BANFF CELEBRATIONS

I have happy memories of early morning jaunts to the Bow River boat house. I would jump into a canoe for an early morning practice for the annual twenty-fourth of May Regatta, which was held in Banff. There were canoe races held on the Bow River or the Vermillion Lake. It was a great time of competition. A "war canoe" race team consisted of both men and women together. This could be a combination of four men, or four women, or a mixed canoe of two men and two women. There were also double canoes races, (men, women, or mixed) as well as single canoe races. Medals and silver cups were given to the winners. Fortunately, I won my share, as result of much practising. Competition came from far away places. Our Banff team also competed at Gull Lake, Alberta in the Canadian Champion Regatta in 1932. There were also rowing races at the regatta, I never took part in anything but the canoe races.

During my years of canoeing and winning, I expect like any teenager, I was beginning to feel that I was pretty good. My father who was an excellent canoeist, had taught me this sport. He soon realized that I needed another lesson, one that might help me through life. He challenged me to a total mile long canoe race on the river. I thought this would be fun, so away we went. My father who had been an excellent athlete, now was not in good condition at that time. As I paddled my best, my father did continuous circles around my canoe. This was a timely, humbling session during the important years of character building.

In the early 1900's visitors were often taken by the early morning train to Lake Louise. There the canoes were unloaded from the baggage car and launched in the river. It was an all day trip before reaching the Mather Boat House in Banff, but one long remembered. My

Bill Green (left) and Gordon Standish (right) with trophies won in Banff canoeing competitions. (Uncle Bill was my father's best man and a special friend in my life)

15

Bow Falls in Banff

By the frozen Bow River, Dorothy Paull is pointing to the place where Miss Gratz would stand and watch Dorothy as she canoed in the river

father used to take some of these trips over the rapids from Castle Mountain to Banff. It was a trip that he took me on and one that is still a thrill to recall. During the high water in the early spring the swollen river was full of floating debris and fallen trees. It took much skill to manoeuvre the canoe around obstacles. The water was fast moving and located just a few miles above the Bow Falls. In later years it looked very risky, but as a young person it just added extra thrills of achievement.

I found out later that while I practised canoeing in the swollen river, I had a guardian teacher, Miss Gratz.

Miss Gratz lived just back of our home. She heard me leave in the early morning on my bike to go to the boat house across the river. Unbeknown to me, she would follow me to the water's edge to make sure I returned safely.

She laughingly said that I had cost her the loss of much early morning sleep. Miss Muriel Gratz was a math and science high school teacher. Besides being a much respected, excellent teacher, she was an ardent outdoor person and took part in many sports including canoeing. I will be ever grateful for concerns shown to me by my school teachers over the years.

My birthday is on July 1 and growing up in Banff, Dominion Day was celebrated with a parade, fireworks and great excitement. It was a real shock when I was old enough to realize that all this excitement was not a celebration for my birthday.

Winter in Banff was the time of the annual winter carnival. A winter week of fun and activities for people from near and far. At one time ice sculptures, made from blocks of river ice, decorated the town for most of the winter. In later years milder climate and chinook winds soon turned them to water so ice carvings became a part of the past. I remember ice palace mazes so large, that one would nearly need a guide to get you through them so you wouldn't get lost.

The Banff winter carnival was guided over the years by many friends and old timers from Banff. Mr. S. Armstrong, was the first president followed by Mr. N. Luxton, Col. P. Moore, and Mr. J. Brewster. Others included, my father Mr. G. Standish, Mr. W. Brewster, and Mr. P. Brewster. Mr. L. Orr was the president the year I became Carnival Queen at the nineteenth winter carnival.

When someone mentioned that I should run for Carnival Queen, I was very hesitant to let my name stand. I didn't have the family support or the finances I would need. However, I did accept and ran against several girls from other areas. I was the most surprised person there when the votes were cast in my favour. It was a thrill and honour to represent my home town the following year in the winter sports.

Banff had a great group of young people called the Outdoor Club. With teachers this group had many outdoor adventures together. When I became Carnival Queen, the support they gave me was tremendous as they were always ready to start and support something.

As Queen, I was expected to attend all sports. With the help of the Outdoor Club, we had a variety of races: snowshoe hurdles, barrel races on snowshoes, and three legged ski races. There were even broom ball games on main street and many more.

One amusing event happened at the Buffalo ski jump. Many of us were keeping warm around a big campfire on a crisp day. We were waiting for

Queen Dorothy

the ski jumping to start, when the announcer's voice came over the loud speaker, loud and clear. "The first jumper will be this year's Carnival Queen, Dorothy Standish." All eyes were on the jump including my own. Over the jump came a good friend of mine, Chess Edwards, dressed in a butterfly skirt. It could have been a bad deal, for as he jumped the skirt flew over his face blocking his vision for the landing. However Chess was an excellent skier and landed safely amid cheers from the crowd.

Being Carnival Queen was a wonderful time for me. I will always be grateful for the support from the town citizens, the Carnival Committee, and the young people. My friends of the Royal Canadian Mounted Police were especially active during these events. They added their scarlet colour as guards of honour during many special occasions.

One of the prizes for being Carnival Queen was a ten day trip to Skoki Ski Camp. It was ten days of skiing, good food, hot toddies, and fellowship with good friends.

Unfortunately, in later years, the carnival was abandoned due to destruction of town property and riotous behaviour from visiting merrymakers.

Ice buffalo during winter carnival carved out of river ice by Charlie Beil

Ice palace made from blocks of river ice as seen, 1993

Queen Dorothy and dog team

Dorothy Standish — carnival queen

Dorothy's winter carnival crown, cups and medals won by Austin and Dorothy (Now donated to the Whyte Museum in Banff)

Dorothy Standish carnival Queen with R.C.M.P. escort

Dorothy Standish - carnival queen, 1935

Banff ski club

Skiers at top of Deception Pass in 1935 on their way to Skoki Ski camp — the winning trip for being Carnival Queen. Dorothy Standish 3rd from the right.

There were many young people who I should mention for their contribution to Banff. Two of them were Mary and Margaret Simpson, daughters of Mr. and Mrs. J. Simpson, noted old timers of Banff.

These very talented young ladies entertained with fancy skating during the winter at many functions. They were special guests at the opening of the artificial ice arena in Calgary. They also had many bookings in 1935-36, not only at our carnival in Banff but in larger cities of Canada and the United States.

The untimely death of Margaret who had married Paul Brown of Cody, Wyoming in 1940 broke up the greatest fancy skating team of the time. Mary and Margaret will always be remembered by their school chums and citizens of Banff as the "Sweethearts of the Rockies."

Banff not only had the Carnival in the winter, and the Regatta in the Spring, but the colourful Indian Days in the Summer as well.

THE NANTON NEWS

Ski-joring behind a fast running horse; mushing with a team of huskies; skating, or ski-ing on the mountain trails all come under the heading of real sport, is the view of Miss Dorothy Standish who reigns as Banff Winter Sports Beauty Queen during this year's season in the Canadian Rockies.

Miss Dorothy Standish, of Banff, is now "Queen Dorothy" of the 1935 Banff Winter Carnival. She was escorted down the aisle at the ballroom where the function took place, knelt at the feet of the late Queen, Miss Violet Davis, of Edmonton, and was crowned by her. Queen Dorothy thanked her subjects and expressed the hope she would make as good a queen as her predecessor on the throne.

A forty-mile ski race, a forty-mile snowshoe race, motorcycle ski-joring, figure skating, ladies and men's hockey, championship speed skating, pony ski-joring, trap-shooting, ski-jumping and many swimming events in the warm pool, will be featured at the elaborate winter carnival at Banff on the week's programme beginning February 14.

Newspaper clipping

Simpson sisters

Indians came from many reservations but mostly from the Morley Indian Reserve. During the Days they set up camp at the Buffalo paddock. Each day, dressed in their wonderful beaded and feathered finery, they would put on a parade. I remember after one parade had started, a rider came riding into town. He told us there would be a short delay because of an emergency. A shelter was erected on the parade route and a baby boy was born. When the parade arrived, there was the proud mother mounted on horse back, showing off her new baby. She gladly accepted payment in return for a look. The parade carried on to the Banff Springs Hotel, where the baby was christened, Banff. Each day following the parade, there was a Pow-Wow with young and old participating.

Many of the Indians became good friends of my father. They called him, "Chief Rain in the Face" because he perspired so much.

The Luxton family were true supporters of the Indians. They built a marvellous museum across the river, to preserve the Indian culture and artifacts. It is a grand place to visit. The Indian Days spurred our interest and respect for the fine work our native people did. We are glad to know that their efforts were preserved.

Indian Days usually followed the Calgary Stampede. As far as I know these events are no longer held.

Gordon Standish "Chief rain in the face"

Indian friends with Dorothy taken in front of the Standish hardware

Start of two mile ski race on Banff Ave. in 1925. Gordon Standish (Dorothy's father on left, Austin, my brother second in line.)

Banff Springs Hotel, an evening shot

Banff Ave.

Banff Ave. in the 30's

BANFF SIGHTS

Our home in Banff was within walking distance of so many interesting sights. We could go to the fish hatchery just above the Bow Falls. There we could study the fish development from the egg to six or eight inch fish that stocked the many mountain lakes. I accompanied my father on many happy fishing trips. We travelled on horseback with a guide and pack train up into the mountain lakes, only accessible by horseback or on foot. Nothing ever tasted better than freshly caught trout fried over an open fire. Some of the mountain lakes were stocked and teeming with rainbow trout.

The building that was the administration building for the fish hatchery

My father decided on a trip to Mystic Lake by horse back. Ike Mills, an outfitter and guide made the arrangements. Ike, his assistants, several adults, one of my school chums, and myself left for a long one day horseback ride. We went through mountain passes to Mystic Lake. It was a beautiful ride with several stops for refreshments. Finally, we arrived at that sparkling lake at the base of a glacier. We erected a long shelter, closed at the top, back and sides, but open to the front. A huge fire was started and kept going all the time. Sleeping bags were unrolled in preparations for everyone's overnight camping. This was followed by a delicious meal of flap jacks and coffee that tasted so-o-o-o good.

The following day everyone wandered off in various directions hoping to be the one to catch the most fish. My school chum and I decided to walk to the mouth of the lake, fed by glacier run off. What a surprise when we got there to find several trout in the icy water on a willow branch and secured to the shore. We were the only group in the area. Who ever caught the trout either forgot them or were scared off as we were in grizzly bear country. Upon returning to camp it was the biggest catch of the day. The fish cooked over an open fire, made a fine meal, and was enjoyed by everyone.

During the night we could hear the bears around the camp. With the large campfire, Ike and his experienced men, we never felt fear.

The following day we were homeward bound. We actually saw grizzly bears who paid no attention to us as we rode by them. It was interesting to learn that grizzly bears have poor hearing and eye sight. Another interesting fact is that they are not disturbed if the wind is blowing away from them. It was still a relief when we passed their area.

Our horses were dependable trail horses and mine was good to ride, especially for an inexperienced rider. As we were travelling along a narrow ledge, with a deep drop on the left and a sharp rising cliff on the right, my horse must have been stung because he suddenly reared. I left the saddle and when I landed I was ahead of the saddle horn, clinging to the poor horse's neck and away we went. I don't know how that sure-footed horse managed, but we passed all the horses on that narrow ledge. Ike was right behind me to catch my mount. That ride didn't last long but I had a sore back for a time from bumping the saddle horn. I felt lucky we didn't go over the bank or have anything worse happen. Except for that, it was a great trip.

Banff is blessed with two natural swimming pools. The water comes out of the mountain at temperatures of 100 degrees fahrenheit and higher. We often would hike to these pools where we would bathe rather than swim.

We made trips in the winter when the roads weren't blocked with snow. This was always a rewarding experience and we enjoyed the hot sulphur pools.

Later when we had a car it was fun to take visitors to these pools for a dip. The pools became famous for curing people crippled from various ailments.

At the Cave and Basin there was a cave where we often went and looked in awe at the bubbling water. As one looked up one could see a hole in the ceiling of the rock covered with stalactites. Legends say that the cave was used by an early Indian tribe. It is still there and one can walk into the cave but the beauty of the stalactites is a thing of the past. I remember as a child the thrill of going into the cave.

Hot Pool where the Indians used to swim at the Cave and Basin

The Upper Hot Springs was the pool my grandparents enjoyed the most. In the early days it was not a very big pool. It was surrounded by a board fence that kept the steam from the naturally hot water inside. Just a very few minutes of bathing were enough unless one was very hardy. I remember fainting on one occasion after staying in too long.

Later the new pool built of Mount Rundle Rock was placed a little further up the mountain. Many people come from far and wide to enjoy it today. The water although still hot coming out of the mountain, is cooled some for swimming comfort. It is fascinating to see the steam rising from the sulphur stream on a cold below zero day.

In those years Banff was a subdivision of the Royal North West Mounted Police later changed to the Royal Canadian Mounted Police. It had an average detachment of twelve to fifteen men and an inspector in charge. Our family members were friends with the members of the force. In those days, children were raised with respect for these men who were serving for the protection of all. Banff was such a beautiful setting for the brick police station and the officers resplendent in their scarlet tunics. No wonder it was a popular place for young ladies to catch the Scarlet Fever.

I have fond memories of a tall fine man, Major Bagley who had a kindly word for me each day we met as I was on my way to school.

R.C.M.P. barracks in Banff

In 1874 under the command of Commissioner French the Royal North West Mounted Police had to get a force together. Their job was to confront two thousand Indian warriors. Many recruits joined and the youngest was Fred Bagley. Son of a former sergeant of the Royal Artillery, he enlisted as a trumpeter and earned seventy-five cents a day. He was an enthusiastic musician and during his service organized more than one band to entertain the men of the local settlers. He returned with the rank of Major. His wife, family, and Major Bagley made their home in Banff. Mrs. Bagley was a special friend of my grandmother's and I always felt a warm concern from them both.

Each year at carnival time a toboggan slide would be built. It was a real treat for the outdoor sportsman. Ski jumping, downhill skiing, and tobogganing were some of the sports enjoyed within easy access to Banff. The boys were jumping on the Tunnel Mountain or Buffalo Ski Jump soon after they could navigate on their skis.

There was little traffic on the streets in those early days. We would ski-jour in the evenings up and down the main street. Usually five or six of us at a time hanging on to different length ropes would ski behind a car. Occasionally the driver would spin around a corner sending the skiers in all directions. Often they would end in a pile in the snow. I look back and realize that the warnings we had from the mounties were for our own good, but we had fun while it lasted. With the arrival of more traffic the time came when this type of sport was no longer allowed on the streets. Our fun was moved to the frozen Bow River. Other than a few bruises, serious injuries were few.

Ski joring on Banff Ave., 1925

There were injuries that will always haunt me. One beautiful Sunday some young people were ski jumping at Norquay. Snow conditions were tricky because of the hot sun and the shadows from the mountains causing a change in snow temperature. A close friend and chum by the name of Sandy Thompson was one of the jumpers. Sandy was an excellent jumper. Because of tricky snow conditions his speed changed as he approached the jump. This caused him to hurdle into space and land so his back was badly broken.

Sandy was a fine student, an excellent golfer, as well as good in all winter sports. During his long illness he excelled in playing chess. Although Sandy lived as an invalid and lived at home for several years he will always be remembered by those who knew and loved him. After our wedding, we took our wedding bouquet to Sandy — our farewell gift.

Another near tragic accident happened one day. Several of us were returning from Norquay down the log shoot after a day of skiing. I was third in line going down the hill. As I arrived at the bottom one of our companions had fallen and badly broken his leg. I managed to stop by heading for the bushes and while doing so broke my skis. It was a bitter cold day and we knew that Stan would soon freeze without help. We all shed our sweaters and what clothes we could do without to wrap around our friend. While some of them stayed to comfort him, I took off on the run to the closest telephone which was about a mile away. I was wearing just a cotton shirt and didn't have the warmth of a sweater. The wind and cold soon took it's toll and by the time I reached the station I was unable to open the door so I kicked it as loudly as I could. I aroused the attention of Mr. Young who after hearing the story immediately called the ambulance. Fortunately the accident happened at the bottom of the hill as at that time there weren't roads up to the ski lodge. The ambulance soon arrived and picked up Stan and his companions. They then stopped to get me, and we all were taken to the hospital. Memories of the freezing coming out of my arms will always be with me. My injuries were nothing compared to what our friend Stan would have to endure. He had both a broken leg and frost bite to contend with. Stan was in the hospital for months but the end of the story is happy. He returned to good health and could walk and ski once again.

 To leave Banff in those early years it was necessary to drive over the Anthracite Hill. This was a narrow mountain road that was often impassable during inclement weather.

 One night I drove with my brother and other companions in the family Dodge touring car over the hill. We were on our way to attend a hockey game in Canmore, the neighbouring town. We were driving along with a bank on the right and a steep drop off on the left when suddenly the whole car shook. A deer, attracted by the headlights jumped off the bank and landed, straddling the car engine. Fortunately, we weren't driving very fast and the car was stopped quickly. The body of the deer was blocking the wind shield. We removed it from the car and placed it by the side of the road. A game warden found the deer the next day and reported that it had so many broken bones it had probably died on impact. This was one of the hazards of driving on the mountain roads in the dark. Many animals are attracted and possibly hypnotized by the bright headlights of an automobile. Except for many dents and scratches to the old car and it's passengers being a bit shaken, everything else was all right. We all felt fortunate that we had not gone over the bank and could continue on to see the hockey game.

 As Banff, nestled in a National Park, its residents seldom heard the sound of firearms. Most residents never learned to handle a gun. I had an unpleasant surprise one morning when I arrived at work. I found the dentist, for whom I worked, and every available man, including my brother had armed themselves with guns. They were out on a man hunt.

The men were after three Doukhobor desperadoes from Arran Saskatchewan, that had been on a rampage of crime. After the Doukhobor men had taken some lives, they arrived at the Banff National Park gate. (As far as I was aware this gate was one of the last projects that my father worked on.) The park attendant had previously received a report of these three men. When they arrived at the park gate, she become suspicious that they were the wanted ones. She notified the Banff Police Detachment, and immediately four mounties hastened to apprehend the wanted trio. Two of the mounties, Sergeant Wallace and Constable Harris, were shot down without having any kind of a chance. That was what had started the man hunt and the three desperadoes had taken off for the hills.

It was an unforgettable day in our quiet mountain resort town. Before it was over, two fine mounties and three young Doukhobor men lay dead. I believe it had all started with an attempt to hold up a garage. It was so sad to end up in bloodshed and the lives of five young men. I was very grateful that it had ended without more deaths. I know there were many nervous citizens out there, untrained to use firearms and searching everywhere possible for the desperadoes.

Banff pioneers. Back row: Mrs. Duncan, Mrs. Clark. Middle row: Miss Foster, Mrs. McKenzie, Mrs. Standish (Dorothy's grandmother), Mrs. Bagley (Major Bagley's wife), Mrs. Haggith. Front row: Miss Tweedy, Mrs. Hind, Mrs. Sibbald

My grandparents brought us up in a happy Christian home, and the early guidance they gave, helped us through many hard days ahead. My grandmother was a strong Methodist and each Sunday was very special. All the meals were prepared on Saturday and the cleaning up done on Monday. Sunday was set aside to go to church and possibly go for a walk in the afternoon. We never even went for a drive. Sundays were kept as the Lord's day and a day of rest.

When I was still at a young age my grandmother suffered a stroke that left her paralysed. Although she lingered for three years, she never spoke again.

We cared for our grandmother at home by each of us taking a turn to look after her. When she was finally released from this life she was just a shadow of her former self. I recall our family doctor saying how pleased he was with the care we had given her as she never had a bed sore. This was something I knew nothing about at the time, but was grateful we had done our best.

Grandpa moved to the coast because of his health and although he returned a few times to Banff for a visit, he spent his remaining years in B.C. He did live long enough to hear that he had a great-grand daughter, Betty. Grandpa passed away in 1939.

Depression years hit Banff along with practically every other part of the country. Formerly thriving businesses either folded or struggled to keep going. Caught in this bind my brother and I were wondering what was the right thing to do. We were young and had very little experience. After much careful thought and planning we decided to turn the family home into a boarding house. In very short order we had eight regular boarders, among whom were several mounties. Some of these mounties became like family and some are still among my best friends. When I look back I wonder how they fared. I was the main course cook and my brother took on the pastry and cake cooking. One friend told us later that he learned in short order to eat and like liver. I believe at that time ten cents bought enough liver for the family, and I know they had it often.

One special Christmas eve I recall a frightening experience. We had been cooking all day and the stove was red hot. The coils ran around the part of the stove where the hot coals heated the water. The kitchen table was piled high with Christmas wrapped homemade candy waiting to be delivered. Our grandfather from B.C. was visiting us for Christmas. He and the boarders had finished their Christmas meal. I had just arrived from the kitchen with the teapot, when there was a terrific explosion. One of the coils had sprung a leak, hot coals and steam filled the kitchen. My brother ran through the fire to turn off the water supply to the coils. Christmas gifts, curtains, and the whole kitchen were on fire. With many hands we were able to put the fire out, but what a mess. There were imprints of the lids from the stove on the ceiling, the explosion was so great. I was also grateful that no one was seriously hurt except for a few burns. I was so thankful that I had missed the full impact of the explosion by just seconds.

This was indeed a busy time. With understanding teachers, we did everything we could. We were able to carry on with our schooling and kept food on the table for ourselves and our boarders.

During the time my brother and I kept boarders we also rented rooms for three dollars a night to tourists. It was hard work for the little we earned for we had to clean the rooms and wash the bedding daily. Often we were left with uninvited guests — bedbugs. Our house had to be fumigated several times during the tourist season.

Mr. Joe Woodworth, a veteran of the 1914-1918 war, was the town's fumigator and had a full time job of getting rid of these pests.

The 1930's were sad years, there were very few jobs available. Many doctors, lawyers, students, and people from all walks of life found themselves without work. They would come to the door asking for a meal in return for some menial chores that they could do.

I have some good memories of these days though as well. I was very busy with an active school life and home chores. I enjoyed the great outdoors, hiking, and canoeing in the summer and then in the winter was the thrill of skiing and skating. My brother also found time for sports and especially excelled in winter sports of speed skating and ski jumping. Summer weekends he and his friends enjoyed scaling the mountains and viewing the panorama of the beauty from the mountain peaks.

One well known ski area in the vicinity of Banff is the Sunshine Ski Area. In the earlier years Mr. Jim Brewster and his wife Dell used to ski into that beautiful area. Several local lads accompanied them, of which my brother, Austin was one. They usually made one or two trips during the winter carrying material that started the first ski lodge called Sunshine.

On one occasion Mr. Brewster brought me the frightening news of a terrifying experience. It was nearing spring and the great danger of snow slides feared. Mr. and Mrs. Brewster were first to go safely over the area. Austin was next and when he was halfway across, the slide started. Austin was an excellent skier and turned his skis downhill ahead of the slide reaching a tree which he wrapped himself around. Fortunately, it was a sturdy tree that withstood the impact of the slide. After the slide passed, Austin was up the tree several feet above the remaining snow. In the Sunshine paper there was an article that Austin Standish had put his name in history forever, by tumbling down Lookout Mountain. There is a ski lift and a mountain named after him. As well, after Mr. and Mrs. Brewster and the other lads that made those first trips.

I am proud that our branch of the Standish name also is a blood relation of one of the North American founders. This was Captain Miles Standish who came over from England on the Mayflower.

Austin and his wife Laurie's family will also carry on the Standish name. Our niece Gayle Louise, and nephews Gordon, Russell, and Brian still make their homes in or near Banff.

Sunshine Ski area just opened shortly before I left Banff, so I have never been there in the winter. However, one summer we went in on the chair lift. We had the opportunity to see the area they had travelled as well as the beautiful new ski area and facilities that they have today. I felt great pride in knowing my brother had a part in its beginning.

Dorothy's husband Tommy, daughter Connie and brother Austin at Sulphur

Austin Standish   *Austin Standish*

Dorothy in front of map Sunshine ski camp, 1984. Dorothy is pointing to where it says Standish lift

Tommy and Dorothy at Sunshine ski area — Standish chair lift in background

Niece Gayle and nephews Gordon, Russell, and Brian Standish in front of Standish hardware

CATCHING SCARLET FEVER

During the Dominion Ski Sports many fine skiers from all over the world gathered to compete. The Royal Canadian Mounted Police were called to help with the handling of traffic up and down the newly built narrow road. The road was built especially to enable people to get to the ski areas on Mount Norquay.

After the Dominion Ski Sports were over, several of the mounties remained in Banff the following year. Their duty was to help with traffic control. Tom Paull was one of the constables who remained, and although I saw him several times, I did not get to know him personally yet.

For a month I was confined to bed with a very bad case of mumps. I stayed in the manse of the minister Rev. Tom Lonsdale, where his kind wife cared for me and nursed me back to health. She had been a nurse during the war years of 1914 -1918.

Once I was well, I went back to work for the dentist Dr. Quigley. I also started to work in the evening as cashier at the Cascade Cafe. I worked with "Freddie" Wing, a lad I had gone to school with. One day, I was having my evening meal, when in came this young mountie, who also had his meals there. He came up to me and said, "Bubbles, will you do something for me?" I wondered what that could be. He went on by saying, "Please don't ever smoke!" I believe at that time he smoked himself, but didn't like to see women smoke. As he didn't know my name he called me "Bubbles." It was because I always appeared happy and to this day he calls me "Bubs."

We began to see each other as long as the working days would allow. I found I had not only caught his eye but Scarlet Fever as well. I was engaged to Constable Tom Paull during the summer of 1937.

Despite both of us working twelve hour shifts we found time for many activities. This included canoeing, and picnics. We danced in the beautiful Banff Springs Hotel dance hall to the music of Mark Kenny. As well we planned for our marriage in the later part of the year.

Const. Tom Paull in Banff

Young single men were often transferred with little notice. One such day my fiance was transferred to Magrath in the southern part of Albert. He was to relieve one of the members for a short time due to ill health. In those days a mountie had to have six years of service and a certain amount of security. Upon completing these criteria, he could then submit an application for permission to marry. We were both plenty concerned as time drew close to our big day. Still there was no word from Ottawa with permission for marriage. I am sure these things held little priority to R.C.M.P. head office, regardless of the anxiety they caused us. However, three days before December fourth we received permission to be married.

After spending most of our saved money on a trip to Edmonton to meet Tommy's family, (his parents, two sisters, and four brothers) we returned to Banff. When we arrived, we found out that Tommy had been transferred to Magrath, Alberta.

The depression made it very hard to get work and my brother, Austin, had gone to Victoria to work on renovations on the Empress Hotel.

It was too cold to live in the suite over the store, so I moved into the home of Grace and Elmer Charleton.

We decided that as soon as Tommy had his six required years in we would quietly get married. After the wedding, I would go south with him to Magrath.

I called my brother and told him about our wedding plans. As he was unable to come back for the wedding, he gave us his blessings.

We asked Tommy's brother Reg and cousin Francis Jackson to stand up with us.

Our Banff friends heard about our plans for a quiet wedding. They said, "No way was I, a Banff girl going off to get married that way." Everything seemed to be taken out of our hands. Grace's wedding veil was made over for me and I acquired a lace wedding dress. While this was going on, our special friend Constable Jim Moffat was at work wiring Tommy to bring his dress uniform. Tommy was told not to ask any questions. Also, they decided that the ushers would wear their scarlet uniforms.

The local girls club decorated the Church and the ministers wife met me at the door to straighten my veil. I entered under the arch of raised arms of the scarlet uniformed attendants. I walked up the isle on the arm of my father. When I looked up at the front of the Church, I was surprised to see my groom in scarlet. Tom was as surprised to see me dressed in white. So, on a cold wintry afternoon in the lovely Mount Rundle Church, surrounded by family and friends we became husband and wife. I started a brand new life — the wife of a mountie. Major Bagley's wife had some parting words for me which I will always treasure.

Dorothy and Austin in front of Mount Rundle United Church, 1936

Two lovely flowers grew side by side

One was love the other his bride

When along came the wind on mischief bent

Into their hearts he sent a rent.

They fell a fighting and both fell dead

Just for the words that should never have been said.

Two lovely flowers in the garden grew

Suppose one was Tom and the other one you

And along came the wind and its merry dance

It'll get you too if you give it a chance.

Dorothy and Tommy Paull's wedding photograph Dec. 4, 1937

CONSTABLE TOM PAULL

Mother and Dad Paull on their 50th wedding anniversary, 1951

Tom Paull was the fourth child in a family of seven. He was the son of Mary and Eben Paull from Columbia Gardens, B.C., just outside of Trail. (This town is no longer in existence). Tom's mother, who was the first postmistress there, named the town Columbia Gardens. The family had a fruit orchard in a fruit growing community which proved unsuccessful due to the Trail smelter being so near.

They then moved east to McCreary, Manitoba to farm, but were driven out by sow thistle. There was no spray or control for sow thistle at that time. The family moved west to Rosetown, Saskatchewan where the family found employment and good schooling facilities. When Tom had finished his schooling, he went on to Regina to join the R.C.M.P. in November 1931.

Left to right: Brother Reg & Joan, Dorothy & Tom, Sister Ebena, Brother Bert & Mildred, Harriet & Brother Cliff, Eva & Brother Harold, Sister Irene & Eldon

After his training he was transferred to the Edmonton and Calgary areas. He was with a full squadron in mounted riot control. This was during the restless unemployment time of the early 1930's.

He was then transferred to Fort Chipewyan which was a two- man detachment. Fort Chipewyan was a very difficult posting. Over a period of ten years many a young constable was transferred there only to stay a year or less. Maybe the hard northern experience was the reason they only stayed such a short time. Tom went to Fort Chipewyan knowing this.

It must have been most difficult for a young man in his early 20's to go from the prairies, to the land of short summers and long cold winters. They depended on boat in the summer and on dog team in the winter for transportation. Knowing all of this he decided to make this northern posting work.

Const. Tom Paull #11201 on riot duty, Spring 1933

One cold winter a patrol was made to Frondulac, 200 miles from Fort Chipewyan. Frondulac was near the east end of Lake Athabasca. Here the lake narrowed to about a quarter of a mile wide and the settlement was on both sides of the narrows.

The special constable, a fine local lad of part Indian decent, not a member of the R.C.M.P., was a civilian employee. He accompanied Tom to the settlement with just one dog team between the two men. They travelled this distance by boat in the summer and by dog team in the winter.

It was too early to be travelling on the lake and their lead dog; "Scottie" seemed to sense this. After a short distance, he laid down on the ice and would go no farther. Tom took his axe and dropped it on the ice near the dog, water spurted up and landed on the ice in front of them. Both men ran toward shore and called Scottie who wheeled the team around and headed for safer ice. There was no doubt in either man's mind that the dog felt the vibration and saved both their lives. Plus he saved the lives of the dog team as well. From that spot on they travelled the shore line taking seven long days to go the 200 miles.

When Tom and the special constable arrived at Frondulac, they found themselves in the middle of an emergency. A young business and family man had been crossing on the ice from one side of the community to the other. Suddenly, his dog team and sled went through the ice. He lost his sled, entire dog team and nearly his own life. Some of his friends on the shore got a rope to him and drug him out of the freezing water until they were able to get him onto some firmer ice. This was when Tom arrived to find the man terribly cold and both of his hands badly frozen. Immediately, they realized that this man was in dire need of medical care. The closest place that they could call for medical help was in Fort Chipewyan. They left the young man in his family's care. As soon as they had given some first aid suggestions, Tom and his companion left quickly for Fort Chipewyan. The temperature had dropped drastically a couple of days before the men had arrived in Frondulac. Now it was safe to cross on the ice instead of having to take the long trip around by land. This time the trip of 200 miles took them three and a half days and three nights, most of the trip was spent running behind the dog team.

As soon as they arrived in Fort Chipewyan, they radioed out for a mercy flight to go and pick up the suffering man in Frondulac. The final word was that the young business man did not loose his hands or any of his fingers. Every one was thankful that he had received medical aid in time.

Tom's first Christmas in Fort Chipewyan was one that he will never forget for many reasons. Coming from such a large warm family group, it must have been a very lonely experience to be so very far from his loved ones. He never had to wonder where he would be on Christmas day before. There was a lack of communication between the Sergeant's wife and the Doctor's wife. Tom did not know which home he would be at for Christmas dinner. In the confusion, Christmas day arrived and he hadn't been invited to either home.

Tom lived in a small two room uninsulated frame cabin, where the heat was from a wood stove. This cabin had been the second man's living quarters at the time.

Tom heard that one of the signal corp members, and his wife were also going to be alone for Christmas day. When he found this out, he invited them to join him for dinner. Christmas dinner consisted of fried caribou, beans, and bannock. As he has always said, he was not there alone. They toasted in the festive season with a drink or two; then thought and talked of happier Christmas's of their past.

As Tom looks back on his northern experiences, winters are what he recalls best. One winter in particular there were several outfits travelling in very severe weather with dog teams. The special constable and Tom were travelling with the group with the R.C.M.P. teams.

At night, after they made camp along the shoreline, Tom and the special constable kicked away the snow from where the dogs would be sleeping. Then they laid spruce bows on the ground for their dogs to curl up on after feeding them frozen fish. Often the others in the party wouldn't take the time to bed their dogs down. So, in the very early hours they had to be up and off to keep their dogs from freezing.

There were always timber wolves in the area. One could tell this by the reaction of the sled dogs who were curled up and hardly moving.

More than once during sub zero weather, that may go as low as -60 degrees fahrenheit or more, Tom would turn the dog sleigh up on its side as a shelter for themselves. They would put spruce bows down for the dogs so they wouldn't be sleeping on the snow. When they were caught out they did what was necessary to survive. They always felt fortunate when they could stay overnight in a trapper's or Indian's cabin. They couldn't afford to pay these people but usually some of their rations were left to thank them for their kindness.

Tom remembered hearing of one incident that made him realize quickly the dangers of winter travelling. It took place on Lake Athabasca.

There was a tractor train consisting of a lead tractor that was pulling two or three freight sleighs plus a caboose across Lake Athabasca. They attached the cars by poles to the lead tractor and then to each other. They used poles instead of chains, in case of an accident and a sleigh goes through the ice. The pole would break so as not to drag in the entire train.

The tractor went through the ice. The pole broke, and severed the tractor from the rest of the train. The tractor operator went down with the tractor but managed to free himself. He came straight up and surfaced at the edge of the ice where the broken pole was. He grabbed the broken pole and dragged himself out onto the solid ice. He ran down the side of the train and hopped onto the caboose to find that the other crew members had already left.

When he ran up one side of the caboose, they were running down the other side of the train, missing each other. When the crew got to the front of the train they saw a gaping hole in the ice where the tractor had disappeared. They were sure the operator had drowned in the icy water. But he had stripped off his clothes and was standing in front of the hot stove trying to warm himself, when his fellow workers returned to the caboose. When they saw their friend, they thought that they were looking at a naked shivering ghost. This was one of the many narrow escapes that happened in the frozen wilderness.

Tom also recalls one summer while the R.C.M.P. boat was anchored in the bay at Gold Field, now Uranium City. A deck hand from another boat came to the R.C.M.P boat by power boat. He reported that one of his fellow deck hands had his foot crushed between the deck of the power boat and the side of a five hundred ton barge. The skipper had been careless in the handling of his boat in a squall. The skipper instructed the lad to try and push the power boat away from the barge, using his feet. Upon hearing this Tom took the R.C.M.P. boat and approached the place of the accident to find the lad in dreadful agony. Tom took the lad to shore and did first aid which eased the suffering.

The captain tried to shirk his responsibility to get the lad out on a commercial aircraft that was in the area. He said that since the R.C.M.P. had taken the lad off his power boat, the lad was the R.C.M.P.'s responsibility. In the end the captain made the arrangements. He did so only after he was informed that if the lad wasn't taken care of, he would end up behind bars.

Tom heard later that the medical help came in time to save the foot and the lad could walk again.

It was after his time in the North that Tommy was transferred to Banff at the time of the Dominion Ski sports.

Fort Chipewyan

Tom's sleigh dogs. Fort Chipewyan, 1935

Trapper's cabin with storage cache in Fort Chipewyan

Harms — (Charged with murder) and Tom in Fort Chipewyan

OUR FIRST POSTING — MAGRATH

Our life together started with an overnight stop in Calgary following the wedding reception. The next morning we drove on to Magrath in our treasured car, a new 1937 Chevy. My husband had served in the north for four years and had accumulated enough money to buy the car. To have one of them was the envy of many in those days.

Tommy kept a secret where we would live upon our arrival. Quite late on that Sunday evening we arrived, loaded with all our worldly possessions, mostly wedding gifts, in front of a cute little bungalow. Tommy carried me across the threshold to a nicely furnished home which was the property of a little old lady, who spent the winter months in a warmer climate. We had electricity and soon had a fire going in the pot-bellied stove in the front room. With love in our hearts it seemed we had everything one could ask for.

A bang at the door in the wee small hours the next morning, summoned my new husband to a safe blowing. With a hasty good-bye he was away. This was the abrupt end to our honeymoon and the start of a new life. All this happened in less than forty-eight hours after becoming a mountie's wife. I learned quickly that law, order, protection of people, and property came first and our personal lives came next.

That first day was something to long remember. I soon found out that the conveniences I had taken for granted in Banff were among some of the things not considered necessary here. Our little house although cosy to the eye lacked running water and bathroom facilities. For the life of me, I wasn't sure where to look for them.

To top it all a blizzard was blowing, and my concerns for my new husband became overshadowed by the necessity to keep the house warm. I soon discovered why our landlady spent the winters in the south. The cute little house lacked insulation, and the curtains were blowing straight out away from the windows in the front room. I spent the first entire day chinking around the windows and doors with newspaper and trying to keep the fire going.

I am not sure what we had to eat when Tommy arrived home safely later that evening. I remember that it was a warmer house, and I was grateful to have had something special to keep busy at.

The Christmas season was approaching quickly. Although we were far from family and friends, we were looking forward to the festive season.

Tommy in front of their first home in Magrath, Alta., 1937

With money given as wedding gifts we purchased a handsome battery cabinet radio. It was beautifully resplendent with a big red bow. We didn't have a tree, and decorations were beyond us that year. Even so, the house looked lovely with our beautiful wedding gifts so recently unpacked. Turkeys were inexpensive and for a couple of dollars we bought and cooked a twenty pound turkey. Somehow as we sat at our first Christmas dinner, happy to be together, our thoughts were with family and friends. Suddenly somehow we didn't have an appetite, and we seemed very much alone.

    People in Magrath were mostly of the Morman faith, a very friendly, kindly people. Their church halls were very popular gathering places for nightly programs and dances. The dance meant entertainment and happiness for most of the people in that area. It meant work for Tommy and loneliness for me. New Year's Eve was among one of those nights I won't soon forget. Tommy was told that he was to attend a country dance in one of the country school houses. He understood that formerly, problems had

Dorothy in front of their first home in Magrath, Alta., 1937

occurred there. Not wanting to leave me alone on New Year's Eve, he decided to take our car, and I could go along. It was nice to be with him, and it wasn't without it's lighter moments.

Several of the young people were outside living it up. When my husband arrived at the school, he started the evening by taking a forty ounce bottle of liquor from them. One of the group was missing at the time. He arrived right after and searched for the bottle with a flashlight. When he spotted it, he thrust a bottle of ginger ale into my husband's hands and said, "Here. Mix it!" He probably never thought that he would be caught so red-handed.

It was nearing four o'clock, New Year's morning when we arrived home, cold and very tired. Quickly, we had a fire going and the chill was just leaving the house when there was a loud bang on our door. All that entered my mind was, "What now!" To our surprise there were about twenty or so young people of the community standing outside. They had been waiting all night for us to return home. They must have realized our need for friends because they brought turkey and refreshments of all kinds with them. What a wonderful and warm way to start our first New Year's Day, something that we have never forgotten.

Early in February, the officer we had gone to Magrath to relieve was returning to his duties and we were transferred to Lethbridge. We left with anticipation of living in a city, but with sadness of leaving our first home. We were still capable of carrying most of our possessions in our little car.

TRANSFERRED TO LETHBRIDGE

Arriving in Lethbridge, finding accommodation was difficult. Finally, we moved into a two-room furnished suite with a semi-private bathroom. The suite had much to be desired, but with wages of $2.25 a day and $1.60 a day living allowance we couldn't afford to be choosy. Our suite consisted of a bedroom which faced the north and was the only room with windows. The dining room, living room, kitchen, and whatever else suited the occasion was all combined in the other room. What must have been a clothes closet at one time served as our cooking area. It included, a two burner gas stove and a small table. There was about a four foot space in between in which to work.

The furnishings were a table, two wooden chairs, and two wicker chairs, (well-roped together). There was an old metal bed with a spring and mattress that could have been a museum piece then. That old bed would be a treasure to those wanting antique pieces of furniture. A painted dresser and two wooden chairs completed the bedroom furnishings. We found only one knife, two forks, and two dishes of various sizes in the kitchen. Our first job on the list was to purchase some dishes and a few cooking utensils, a start to acquiring household necessities.

I still remember the look on my brother's face when he called in to see us one day. I guess our home didn't look too luxurious to him, but we were grateful for what we had.

Life for a young constable was a monotonous routine of shift work which consisted of twelve hour shifts. Most of Tommy's responsibilities consisted of guard duty to the entrance of the R.C.M.P. compound. I also found life monotonous those first few weeks with little to do and no friends yet. It seemed that even my attempts as a cook failed. The extent of my cooking success was the main course of the meal. I tried my best at yeast buns. This was a mistake, as they ended up resembling billiard balls by both size and hardness.

I thought I'd make Tommy's favourite dessert, pumpkin pie! All seemed well except time ran out to have it cool for dinner. I brought in a pan of snow and set the pie in it to cool. Since this special dessert was to be a surprise, I had the pie well hidden in the bedroom. I went to bring him the pie, which looked so delicious when I put it in the bedroom. All I produced was buckets of tears, when I found the pie submerged in the melted snow.

Both Tommy and I were in our sunless home for a whole, entire week due to a bad dose of flu. As soon as we felt better, we decided to look for something better. By the end of March, we had found and arranged to move into a small house at the corner of two lanes. It was within walking distance to Tommy's work. We now had a front room, a bedroom, kitchen and most important of all a bathroom of our own. This was a luxury we hadn't enjoyed since leaving Banff. We bought our first furniture, a chesterfield, two chairs, a box spring, and good mattress. We also ordered a bedroom suite that was to arrive in a month. With a card table and chairs that belonged to us, there was not a place in Lethbridge that looked so beautiful. We even had a small fenced yard with visions of a garden when spring arrived.

One day my husband arrived home with a bulging and moving pocket. I was surprised to find out that he had brought the cutest little Boston Bulldog puppy home. It was to provide some company for me while he was away. We decided almost immediately that "Puggy" was the most appropriate name. He seemed to fall in love with us as fast as we did with him. Things were different that first night, in spite of all we did for him, it was not enough. He cried so loud and so long that it seemed like nothing would ever make him happy. Finally, with a hot water bottle under his pillow, and our alarm clock wrapped in a towel ticking near by Puggy, he got quieter. He found the security and warmth he needed. Finally we all slept!

Lethbridge in those days wasn't the beautiful city that irrigation has made of it today. The country was dry and arid. Although we sometimes took a lunch we had difficulty finding a nice place for a picnic.

Every cent had a place, but each pay day we managed to put ten cents away so we always had some money. Each pay day we would fill the gas tank of the car. We used to drive to the top of the Lethbridge hill for our outings and then to conserve gas we would coast down again. One such time a sudden shower occurred and with so much dust in the air the rain came down in mud. The window clouded over before we could get the motor started. Soon the wind shield wipers stuck to the window. We never tried to coast much after that scary experience.

NORTHERN POSTING — FORT McMURRAY

It seemed as if before we were settled, my husband arrived home with some news. He had been asked if he would go north to Fort McMurray. Northern postings were always volunteer, but with Fort McMurray being still within the Alberta boundary this was not so.

Since Tommy had already served time in the north, he was given time to think the move over. The north seemed to be such a fascinating place. I recalled some of the stories I had heard from the patrols that had been to the northern part of Lake Athabasca. Places including Stony Rapids in Frondulac and Goldfields in Saskatchewan (the latter presently known as Uranium city). As well as areas north down the Slave River to Fort Fitzgerald, Fort Smith, and down to Fort Resolution. There were also trips made up the mighty Peace River, which emptied into the Slave River. They continued down river to Fort Chipewyan, where Tommy had spent nearly four years.

Tommy told me about his trip to Fort Chipewyn to replace a constable who had come out due to illness. He was young and inexperienced to the ways of the north, and it was all a challenging experience to him. After a slow trip on the train to Waterways, Tommy boarded the big paddle wheeler S.S. Echo. He continued the trip down the mighty Athabasca River. There were only three passengers so they had the royal treatment of dining at the captain's table for the entire trip. The Echo was pushing a 500 ton barge in front. Three hundred ton barges were held in place by heavy ropes on either side of the ship. The barges were loaded with freight for the far north. It was one of the first trips in after the long winter, since the spring breakup. There was little sleep during that first trip, with the breath taking beauty of the early spring breaking into its loveliness. Combined with the amazing capability of the ship crew maneuvering the ever changing channels.

This made a spell binding experience for a first time passenger. I could almost imagine the beauty that he saw from the bridge. I visualize the day slipping into twilight and almost at once breaking forth into another day. While he listened to the swish, swish of the paddle wheel as it drove that big boat and its cargo into the northern waters.

Those first barges loaded with supplies of fresh vegetables and fruit must have been a welcomed sight to those northern dwellers. The stories of rationing fascinated me and I wondered if I would do as well as they did.

The summer patrols, made mostly in the R.C.M.P boat, which were double ended and powered by a marine type engine. Although often plagued by mosquitoes and no-see-ums, (an almost undetectable minute-sized little insect with the bite of a wasp), the beauty experienced was breath taking. The northern summer patrols unfolded the beauty that words seemed inadequate to describe. These stories made me wish I had been a part of it.

The northern winters were long and cold. During this time patrols were made with dog teams. I recall hearing about Scottie the lead dog of the R.C.M.P dog team. This dog who would never be a pet, at times had to receive severe lessons of obedience. Scottie will always be remembered and spoken of with affection and respect. A big day trip with a dog team was between thirty and thirty-five miles and usually in below zero temperatures.

While on a trip going to investigate a suspected murder case, they travelled non stop for ninety miles. It took two days and a night, with only brief stops every three or four hours to rest the dogs. Each dog was given a quarter of a fish to keep up their energy. During this time the drivers would boil a pot of tea and have some bannock, cheese, and jam. What endurance tests these trips must have been and all for the big wages of $2.25 a day. This case would make a story in itself. It involved a long, hazardous trip in weather, 30 or 40 degrees below zero fahrenheit, as they travelled over ice and bush trails. This combined with the effort of mounties, Indian guides, and Northern Bush pilots to bring a man to justice who had caused death and panic in the Northern wilderness.

I recall stories of the beautiful long summer days when one could read in the midnight sun, and the stories of long winter days. Many of the cold winter nights were alive with the ever changing northern lights. Although they do not make a noise, one could imagine them snapping as they flashed in many hues across the sky.

Midnight sun and moon — Arctic coast

Dog teams leaving Fort McMurray, 1986

Fort McMurray, 1939

I was told of so many memories of my husband's experiences in the north. It was small wonder that we decided to take the posting to Fort McMurray in northern Alberta. We thought it would be a further challenge and maybe a happier place than the dry southern part of the province.

Fortunately for us Tommy had recently passed through Fort McMurray on his way out of the north. Upon accepting the move he was told he would be going to a furnished detachment. He was to sell all of his furniture in preparation for the move. Of course after a recheck on this, they acknowledged that Fort McMurray was not a furnished place. Immediately, we began a taxing job of crating all of our few treasured pieces of new furniture for the long trip. We weren't living in the age of easy moves as all the crating and packing had to be done by ourselves. Everything, was packed in the R.C.M.P. moving van, a far cry from the up to date moving vans of today.

It seemed to be a long time before we ever saw our bedroom suite that we had ordered. It had been redirected to our new destination.

We also had our first and, I think, our last experience of buying on time (or credit). This was a new dining room suite, a real beauty, we thought. It included a table, four chairs with red leather seats and a buffet. We paid the deposit required and before we had finally paid the last payment we had almost paid double the price. From that time on we always bought as we could afford it. A good decision for us as we never did like the dinette suite with the memories attached to it.

The time of departure arrived late in May. With high hopes and dreams of excitement we headed north to Edmonton in our own car. One hard decision that we had to make when we decided to move north was to sell our lovely car. We sold it in Calgary, but the new owners allowed us to drive it to Edmonton to deliver it. There just wasn't much cash in those days so we took a credit note. It was an excellent idea at the time to know we could be sure of a car in the future.

We had time to take a day to drive to Banff and say good- bye to all our friends and family. It was nice to see my home town again in a beautiful time of year.

Our wee pup, Puggy was now very much a part of the family and almost in full control. Puggy was a very good traveller

Puggy, comfortable in a little crate, looked a bit doubtful as we put him in the baggage car all alone. When the, "All Aboard" was sounded, with farewells said, we were on our way to a new life in a new part of this large country. The Northern Alberta Railway was anything but luxurious, with few of the comforts of today's rail transportation. The train lacked a dining car or comfortable state rooms. This was corrected by all of the wonderful care we were given by the train personnel. It didn't take us long to notice the Northern friendliness.

There were many passengers, some on their first part of the journey to far places in the north. Some, like ourselves, the journey would end at the Waterways, the end of the railway north. These passengers included police officers, prospectors, and missionaries. Although we didn't realize it yet some of these people would play a part in our Northern experience.

The train which moved slowly north rode on tracks laid over muskeg country. Rough would hardly describe the journey which took two days and a night to travel the 300 miles of Northern wilderness. Occasionally the train would stop to take on fuel and water. Then passengers would get off to take a walk and stretch their legs. We would dash to the baggage car where our poor little pup shivered in bewilderment. Puggy, was so happy to find that he wasn't altogether forsaken. On some of these stops, I understood that some fishing was done. Proof that we were already in the country where no one hurried.

I recall a story told to describe the slowness of the train. A lady nearing her time of delivery kept asking the conductor when they would arrive at their destination. After several times of reassuring her that they would get there in due time, he asked her why she was in such a hurry. She said that she was soon going to have a baby. The conductor cautioned her that she shouldn't be travelling in that condition. The lady then said that she wasn't in that condition when they had started on the train. Just a story, but a descriptive way of showing that northern travelling was slow and rough.

The train pulled into Waterways, the end of the steel, on a beautiful day mid May. We travelled the remaining few miles to Fort McMurray by taxi to the R.C.M.P. detachment, our home for the next four years.

Puggy was so happy to be able to run in a big, well enclosed yard. Our new home had a small screened in front porch. This entered into the living room and dining room divided by an archway in the centre. The main heat for the house was a big circulating coal and wood heater. Straight off the dining room was the office with a room off the back for extra sleeping space for overnight visitors. In one corner there was a cell. It was constructed from two by fours on the flat and didn't look like the most secure detention area. Also off the dining room was the kitchen. We had one bedroom and a path out the back door to a little building in the back yard. A stairway in the dining room led to an unfinished attic.

The house was in a terrible state. The attic was alive with moths where old fur pelts had once been stored. Wall paper was torn and hanging in tatters on the wall showing the lath strips beneath. There were square holes cut in the floor, apparently to let in some heat from a small stove in the dugout beneath the house. Puggy had satisfied his curiosity quickly after falling through one of these holes, causing a commotion and requiring one of us to rescue him.

That first day was all it took to dash to pieces our excitement and happiness about transferring to Fort McMurray. The inspector and his wife dropped in on their way to Fort Smith. They were on their way to supervise the transfer of the man who had just left Fort McMurray. While the men were busy in the office, the inspector's wife joined me in looking at what was to be our home. With indignation and tears she asked her husband how they could send a bride like me to a dump like that. It took but a quick look to condemn the house. Which meant, for the summer our home would be the one small room off the office until the house had been completely redone.

We had room to put up our bed, have two easy chairs, and our radio in there. It was some time before our carefully packed treasures were unpacked, except a few necessary items that we needed while camping "temporarily."

We were assured that though our house didn't have any modern facilities we had the best well in town. We had been told that one day we might even have electricity.

For some reason my predecessor was anxious for me to be a loner. She advised me that a police officer's wife just couldn't make close friends. This was something of a shock and a surprise to me. I was one who had always enjoyed the companionship of many friends. After mentioning this, my husband soon reassured me that I was not to pay any attention to such a suggestion.

I am glad to report that the friends that I made those four years were some of the finest that I would ever make. There was to be a tea party that first day and the invitation was to be passed on to me by the former member's wife. I didn't find out about it until a few days later. I felt more pity for the other wife than bitterness and hoped that the northern experience wouldn't embitter me as it had done to her.

Life that first spring was too busy for us to worry about our start. Tommy had inherited several unfinished files which kept him busy. We were still in depression times and many poor chaps rode the rods to the end of the steel looking for work. After finding nothing to do, they would just sit and wait for the next train south. These were days of unrest and many a night my husband would patrol the jungle. (A term used in the depression times for areas used for camping and sleeping of the transient people). He helped where he could, while patrolling the area.

We had a big garden space and had to move quickly to dig it and get it ready for planting. Being a mountain girl, a garden was a new experience. I was very thankful that my friend and husband had been raised on a farm and could guide me in preparing and planting the garden. The days in June were long, the sun hardly dipped before it rose again. It seemed as if we could almost see the garden growing. I used to pull up thirty to forty pails of water from our well to water our garden. I learned to can peas, beans, tomatoes, and many other vegetables from the recipes and experience shared through common conversation with the northern women.

Fort McMurray home and R.C.M.P. office, 1938

Tom in police canoe on the Sny — Fort McMurray, 1938

Tom at Fort McMurray in front of home and R.C.M.P. office, 1938

Dorothy and Tom in Fort McMurray, 1939

One day although a storm had been threatening, several of the ladies decided to go saskatoon berry picking and I joined them. I had been promised by the ladies that the best place to pick berries was on the island. This piece of land was surrounded by the waters of the Sny, the Clearwater, and the Athabasca rivers. Tommy took us across the Sny in the police canoe and arranged to return to meet us at a specified time.

Once on the island we found to get to the berry patch we had to cross over much deadfall. It was in most places piled high off the ground. Carrying our picking pails we made our way, careful not to fall. When suddenly I was surrounded by wasps, I must have disturbed a nest. They were up my pant leg, in my face, all around me. They stung me in many places before I was able to get away from them. We finally managed to climb over the remaining deadfall. We came to a clearing in the centre of the island where we found some mud to put on to ease the stinging. I was so sore and it really did help.

Just about then a violent electric storm hit the island. Besides the fear of the storm, we were drenched. However, we had come to pick berries and berries we picked, until we each had our pails full.

It was getting to the time for Tommy to pick us up. After the heavy rain we knew we couldn't cross that deadfall of timber again; nor did I want too! We decided we would walk around the island to the appointed spot, little knowing that it was so far. It was hard going and some of us spilt our berries. We arrived at the Athabasca River shore a bedraggled group.

We hailed an Indian fishing boat and asked if they would send word to the mountie of our whereabouts. They did better than that. With difficulty they got us into their boat, and then landed us safely at the Sny wharf.

We arrived hours late of our planned meeting time to my worried, furious mountie, who had felt so helpless not knowing what had happened to us. His relief at finding us safe and sympathy for my wasp stung body, soon helped him over come his anger. Although, Tommy was worried, he soon started teasing me about a full day of northern berry picking and an empty pail.

(I believe the island is now cleared and is a golf course in the modern thriving community of Fort McMurray.)

Soon after our arrival in Fort McMurray we noticed that a little house was being built next door. We discovered that our new neighbours were a newly married couple from southern Alberta. They had travelled to the north on the same train as we had. We visited back and forth, and admired this couple who had little but dreams as they built their small house. They hoped that something would turn up to supply their needs so they could make a living.

Transportation for the police was by the waterways only. They travelled in a twenty foot canoe with an outboard motor mounted on the right side of the stern. When there were emergencies, a taxi was hired to travel the only three miles of road to Waterways. Trips were made in the canoe up and down the Clearwater and the mighty Athabasca rivers. Joining these two rivers was a picturesque back water called the Sny. It was on this strip of water that boats were anchored and sea planes landed to refuel. These planes were piloted by the famous bush pilots going to and from the north.

Not long after our arrival, on a beautiful spring day tragedy hit. A couple of transient fellows helped themselves to an Indian birch bark canoe and pushed it out into the deep water. Local residents called warnings to them from the shore, among those calling was my husband. Heeding the warning, one chap returned to land. The other head-strong fellow, thinking he could master the cranky water, pushed off to his death. Before any of the onlookers could reach him, he had disappeared into the swift and murky current and was swept away. Hours of dragging and searching were to no avail. Gloom settled in on all as they thought of the helplessness of the situation.

The spring was beautiful. The long, long days made the trees and shrubs burst out into leaf before our eyes.

It was important that our little dog Puggy be taught obedience to heel or he wouldn't last long in the land of the husky dogs. We would enjoy the lovely mile walk to the Sny in the evenings. We tied Puggy to the end of a long stout cord. At first the command "heel" meant nothing to a curious pup. When he showed no signs of hearing us or obeying our command a good pull on the cord would send him head over heels. He was a smart puppy, and this only happened a couple of times before he received the message. We spent many happy hours training Puggy. He made a name for himself with his tricks which included: saluting, quick marching on his hind legs, dancing, chewing gum, and saying his prayers. Years later one young mountie, who spent some time in McMurray with my husband, wrote to us saying he could still hear my husband say. "Pray Puggy, pray. Damn it Puggy pray." It really wasn't that bad but was a job to teach him to keep both eyes closed at the same time.

We were still in the one room off the office, when my husband had to be away for a few days. I was left alone. Puggy slept on a pillow between the office door and the pot-bellied stove. The door to our room was on the other side. The first night I was alone that little dog wouldn't settle down until he had dragged his pillow to the doorway. He seemed to feel the need to protect me or maybe he felt the need to be protected. As he grew he became all muscle as only a little Boston bull dog could. Following a commotion in our backyard we would look out to see Puggy sailing over a six foot fence. Puggy would be hanging onto the tail of an uninvited husky who was doing its best to get away from that little ball of fury.

In the early summer it was necessary to go down the Athabasca to Indian encampments to pay their yearly treaty pay. A considerable sum of money was being carried, so this was the reason the police became involved. The treaty money was the annual payment in cash to all treaty Indians. This was the agreement when the early treaty was signed in the time of Queen Victoria. Since we were still not able to move into our house, we decided that I would go along on this journey. It was a trip that I will forever remember. Supplies and fuel was loaded for the trip. Accompanying us on the trip was an Indian agent doctor and his interpreter. It was very hard to describe the beauty of the scenery on the trip. Although, it was anything but a pleasure trip for Tommy. Sitting in one position, hour after hour, Tommy steered the large canoe from the side. Manoeuvring the canoe through the ever changing channels was tiring and nerve racking. We would stop occasionally for a short time, long enough to boil water, have tea, and eat lunch. These were welcomed rest stops.

We stopped at the following Indian villages to pay treaty money: Fort McKay, Poplar Point, and Embarrass Portage. This was an extremely exciting time for the Indians and they gathered from far and near. While the men were busy, I wandered amongst the camps. It was interesting to watch the women make stew in the large metal pots hanging over open fires. I admired the little babies, snug in their moss bag hammocks, hanging between two trees. They were naturally rocked to sleep by the gentle breeze. The women were friendly. Although we had a language barrier, smiles mean the same in any language. It helped me feel that I was a part of the north. The first day was long. It was nearing midnight when we finally found a place to camp. We were about fifty miles north of Fort McMurray, near Bitumount. This was a site of an extensive experimental plant which extracted oil from the tar sands. It had once been a very busy operation but now stood quiet.

We put our sleeping bags well up on the bank, hung our mosquito nets in place and settled in. My husband, exhausted, soon fell asleep, I on the other hand was not so lucky. A few mosquitoes had managed to get inside our netting. With their buzzing and the steady buzzing of the millions outside the netting, they did not make for good sleeping partners. I decided that if I couldn't sleep at least I could keep them from stinging the skipper. I spent the night swatting the little pests. The northern sky was full of stars, yet it never seemed to get dark.

Suddenly, I heard a chug, chug sound in the distance, growing stronger as it came closer. Soon right in front of our sleeping area appeared a huge paddle boat with three or four barges captained to the front and sides of the boat. All the port holes were ablaze with light, and it looked like a floating palace. As it passed from sight, I recalled the stories told to me about this beautiful river boat. It carried both passengers and freight up and down those northern waterways.

Paddle boat and barge — Fort Chipewyan

The drone of mosquitoes outside our netting got louder and louder. When the sun finally rose, the mosquitoes were so thick that it looked like a moving grey mist. Finally the heat of the morning and the whine of the insects woke up the sleeping men. We quickly made a fire to discourage the insects and cooked our breakfast. I realized that first night out in the wilderness, how an unprotected person would perish in the north country. If the person was not harmed by wild animals, then he would be driven crazy by the troublesome insects.

When our trip was over, the agent doctor and his interpreter carried on north, with another R.C.M.P. patrol from Fort Chipewyan. We then headed towards home. The trip home was much slower, as we were travelling south against the natural current. The weather remained beautiful and each day presented a new thrill for me. On our return we stayed overnight at Fort McKay.

While there, we were the guests of the Hudson Bay manager and his wife, Mr and Mrs. Bob McDermid. Everyone called Mrs. McDermid, Granny. These people seldom had company and made us feel like royalty. Granny was well known for her tea cup reading abilities. Later that night I realized that she had a special talent. Our tea cups were similar, the message in both was a puzzling one. My husband was to receive instruction to go and get someone. Although he knew where the person was he would be unable to get him. Knowing Granny's reputation in fortune telling, we couldn't help think about this and wonder what it meant.

In the morning we paid our farewells with the knowledge that we would see them in the fall. After their retirement, they would be moving to Fort McMurray. They would then be near neighbours of ours. Upon arriving home that night we found the answer to the tea cup reading. In the official mail from Edmonton there was a warrant to arrest a young chap who had drowned in the Sny. My husband knew where he was but could do nothing about it. Later they discovered the body miles down the river. My husband had to make the long journey there on his own to identify the young man and arrange burial.

Midsummer found our living quarters freshly wall boarded, painted, and ready for us to move into. At last, we could uncrate our furniture. For the first time we could see our new bedroom furniture. It finally had caught up with us. After getting it out of the packing boxes, there in front of us was this "new" furniture, all nicked and battered.

We decided that we would rather not have the circulating heater in the middle of the front room. My husband spent hours and hours of hard work enlarging the smaller hole under the house, to make a two room basement. This enlarged area was large enough to put the furnace in. The piped heat to each room gave us very comfortable living quarters, for the four years of our posting, even in the coldest of weather. That room also had enough space for a chemical toilet, a great luxury for the coming winter. The other room which was accessible by ladder was a dandy spot for storage, where we kept our food supplies.

This was our second home which didn't have any kind of plumbing. We had a pail for fresh drinking and cooking water. It wasn't far to our well, which was just outside the back door. I guess, in a way we did have running water, if we needed water we just ran out and got it. Our sewer system consisted of a "slop bucket" that I detested keeping clean. It had to be carried out and dumped regularly. Our well was the best in town but gave out that first summer.

One day when the pail was pulled up it had oil floating on the top. The oil from the tar sands had seeped into our well, as it had done with so many other water sources. From then on we had to carry our water from quite a distance. Our pail in the well became our refrigerator. We brought water by the barrel for washing, dishes, bathing, and cleaning. We kept the reservoir in the kitchen wood stove full and while the fire was going we had hot water.

Our house was warm and comfortable. Our pup, Puggy soon decided his special place was under the kitchen stove.

Each day seemed to bring with it new experiences. A mountie's family could always plan their day in the morning, but it didn't mean that the day would go the way it was planned. One day while working in the kitchen I heard someone enter the front door. Thinking it was my husband Tommy, I called out a "Hi, there!" All was silent. Deciding I should go and check, I found a stony faced Indian and his wife, sitting placidly on our new chesterfield. They sat there quietly waiting for Tommy, thinking they had entered the office.

Our occasional "lodgers" that were in the cell required meals. This has been the subject for much teasing in many a conversation. When a meal for a prisoner was asked for I prepared three servings of our meal. I placed one on a neat tray complete with our dishes, a knife, and a fork. I learned a lesson in a hurry, that you didn't include dangerous eating tools. From then on they would get the same food as we had. Complete with a tin plate and a spoon with meat already cut up. For these meals we received the equivalent of a restaurant meal. Which was about thirty-five cents for breakfast and fifty cents for the other meals.

The R.C.M.P. had rations which they gave to Treaty Indians as they needed it, but we were not on rations. We bought case loads of canned fruit and vegetables. We had them shipped in from Edmonton. Other than that we bought fresh things from the local stores. Meat was a problem in the summer months due to lack of refrigeration. Meat would come in on the train each week. For the first few days we would be fortunate to have fresh meat.

I recall hosting what turned out to be an upsetting and embarrassing dinner party. One evening we invited the doctor, his wife, and family over for a meal. We bought a lovely looking rolled roast of beef. As the heat penetrated the centre of the roast, this terrible odour of spoiled meat penetrated and filled the house. We managed to find the town butcher and our guests fared on bologna. I seemed to be the only one upset. We found our fine guests very understanding. Since they were seasoned northerners, possibly they had experienced similar circumstances before.

Fresh berries in the summer were bountiful and included saskatoons, blueberries, raspberries, and chokecherries. They grew in abundance and fresh vegetables were found in nearly every garden. The winter months found us fairing chiefly on canned vegetables and oranges brought in by the caseload. The winter made it possible to have good meat including caribou and ducks, wrapped and frozen, then kept in the northern natural refrigerator.

The hot days of summer were fading into shorter days and longer nights. There was an unusual nip in the air for September. The luscious green foliage changed into gorgeous shades of orange, red, and yellow.

Our neighbours had finished their house and were working on a snowmobile project. Their hopes were to make their living by hauling freight during the winter. They were expecting a baby in their home. Although we were very happy for them, we knew that they must have felt far from their families at such a time.

Granny and Bob McDermid had moved to Fort McMurray and wanted to get settled before freeze up. I called in to welcome Granny to the area. I stayed for a cup of tea, hoping that she might suggest reading my teacup again. After a lovely visit she picked up my cup, took a look, and replaced it on my saucer. I questioned her with my eyes. She told me that she never read tea cups for anyone who was expecting a baby. I was sure she had made a mistake, it must be my neighbour. No, she was right, a new member would be coming to our house the following spring.

One cold fall day, we received word at the detachment that a body was found. It was in a boat some one hundred miles down river, foul play was suspected.

Preparations were made for the trip and for the first time I prepared bannock to go in a grub box. (Bannock is similar to baking powder biscuits but richer, and after it is baked it is quickly frozen. Bannock has a lot of shortening in it, so it thaws quickly over an open camp fire.) The next morning I walked to the shore of the Sny and watched as the police boat disappeared around the island. Tommy didn't know how long the trip would take or what they would find. It was the longest week I can ever remember.

Cold was setting in over the north. The local people were talking about the six months of freeze-up expected to start any day. Planes which landed on pontoons during the summer months were now heading south to wait for freeze-up. Then they would return on skis. One day passed into another.

I recall long days of being alone in the detachment and doing what I could for those who called. I spent many sleepless nights, but still no report of anyone seeing the police boat. The last plane had gone south, and I was feeling hopeless as I washed up my evening dishes. Suddenly, I thought I heard the sound of a motor. I ran outside to listen but there wasn't a sound. After thinking I heard it a couple more times, I thought I was loosing my mind. Finally, I couldn't stand it any more. I bundled up and hiked down the dark road to the shore of the Sny. The last part of the walk, I practically flew for sure enough I had heard the motor. It was loud and then faded as the canoe travelled in and out among the islands. Tommy was towing the boat in which the body lay awaiting the viewing of the closest coroner who lived in Fort McMurray.

The next day the river was frozen over and six months of freeze up started with water transportation at a stand still. Communication with the outside world was by the one passenger train a week. Mail received was answered immediately and sent out by return mail. With the busy summer over, everyone seemed to settle into winter activities. I belonged to the I.O.D.E. Fort McMurray chapter. Although small in number we kept active working on several community projects. To swell our funds we decided to have a dance, a very formal social event of the fall. Orders were sent to Eaton's mail order catalogue for gowns and all the necessary accessories. The dance was open to everyone. A large crowd gathered in the small hall to enjoy the gathering, and dance to the piano music provided by our talented banker, Mr. Thorpe.

I wore my wedding dress; it was just one year old. One of our friends looked lovely in a long white dress with red polkadots and white shoes. We felt in the festive mood as we entered the hall. There wearing the similar dress with red polka dots as shown in the catalogue was one of the native girls. On her feet were moccasins and her black hair quite unkempt hanging in braids down her back. We laughingly decided that they had both made a good choice. Some of the sparkle had gone out of the evening for our friend.

For our snowmobile freighting neighbour next door, trips down the river took him away from his wife for long periods of time. His wife spent as much time with us as possible, and we were very happy to have her with us. It was on such a day that we walked with her to the hospital. Where soon after her husband had returned from a trip, she gave birth to their first little daughter. This little girl became very special to us; for not only is she my name sake, but she is also our god child. We felt a special closeness to this little family who were our neighbours.

Before winter, the luxury of D.C. electric lights were introduced into our community. The electric plant was located just across the road. Our quiet life was changed by the full roar of the throbbing motor. The conveniences of the light plant were most welcome. We had electricity Monday and Tuesday mornings, for washing and ironing for those who could afford the cost of twenty- five cents a kilowatt.

We continued using the flat iron heated on the stove and the wash board with the tub. We were looking forward to a wringer- washing machine before spring. The lights stayed on until ll:00 P.M. so it was a great help during those long dark days of winter. We enjoyed our battery radio set immensely. During those long evenings we listened to broadcasts. The "Call of the North," was especially entertaining as we listened to messages to the far north. Occasionally, we would hear messages to local residents or to ourselves.

Our first Christmas in the north was a festive affair held at the home of the local druggist, Mr. and Mrs. Walter Hill. Mrs. Hill had arrived as a bride from London, England to Fort McMurray. She had made a home there for her husband and two sons. Christmas meal consisted of turkey and all the trimmings. The evening finished with family participation in games while movie cameras were in evidence trying to capture the happy times on film. Each family had arranged to have a turkey for Christmas. Sundays during the winter found us having Christmas all over again at one home or another. We enjoyed laughs together as we watched the movies taken on the previous occasions. As we look back at these movies it seems as though we were always eating. The memories of those happy occasions will always be treasured.

Friendships that we made, became strong, and we still keep in touch. Our friends, the Hills, still live in Fort McMurray where they owned and operated the drug store. They had celebrated more than sixty years of marriage, all of which have been in that beautiful northern village.

Fort McMurray has changed into a thriving booming oil community, and the Hills are proudly watching a third generation that is nearing graduation in pharmacy.

With a baby on the way I started to prepare for the big event. Fortunately, I had taught myself to knit, but not having a woman's guiding hand in the earlier years I had no knowledge of sewing. I ordered yards of flannelette and baby clothes patterns from the catalogue. With the help of a treadle sewing machine, I started to work. I carefully hemmed the diapers before starting on the nighties.

Fortunately, I hadn't advanced too far with them when one day a friend, our banker's wife, Mrs. Thorpe, called for tea. Having a small family herself, she was interested in what I was making. I knew by the look on her face, that she was feeling pity for the wee baby that would wear the nightie. I was sewing the nightie with raw seams. I learned that day under her guidance how to make flat seams, and how to read a pattern properly. This was the start to years of required sewing that followed. Rubber pants were unheard of garments, and we knit little pants called soakers. The soakers were worn over the diapers. The winter passed quickly, with the knitting of several pairs of soakers, several knitted sweater outfits plus the items I had sewn.

Before we knew it the spring break-up was approaching. Planes that travelled on skis during the winter waited in Edmonton until they could return to the north on pontoons. We looked forward to spring breakups with mixed emotions of excitement and fear. Excitement, knowing the end of a long winter had come at last, and fear for the havoc a bad break up could cause.

Sweepstakes were held, to guess the exact time and date that the ice would go out right at Fort McMurray. Although the prize money wasn't any huge amount, everyone hoped he or she might have the winning ticket.

As the weather got warmer farther south, the melted snow and ice would cause the swollen rivers to rush north. The rushing water would hit the frozen rivers causing great pressure on the ice and the water would break through with a thunderous roar. It would often pile up large pieces of ice far up on the river bank. A particularly bad break up could put trappers and other northern dwellers in danger of loosing their homes. They often had tree houses and other cashes for such emergencies.

The first break-up that I was in the north for, but missed seeing, happened before midnight in early May. Old timers were sure the ice would go out that night, and I was anxious not to miss it. Along with several friends we bundled up warmly and walked to a safe high point over looking the Athabasca River. It was a bright crisp moonlight night. Everything looked beautiful but eerie as we waited in anticipation, listening to the rumblings of moving ice in the distance. After several hours of waiting, we were chilled right through. We headed home to make a hot cup of coffee. As we reached our gate, we heard a thunderous roar. We had missed seeing the breakup by just those few minutes.

The next day the water was running free. The river being full of huge pieces of ice, would carry on north to continue the break up pattern. Ice was thrown ten to fifteen feet above the river level and for a quarter of a mile up onto the bank. Here it melted slowly for the next couple of weeks as the warm days of spring approached.

During my second spring in the north in early June my mother-in-law arrived. It was so wonderful to have her and to see one of our family for the first time that year. The weather was warm and beautiful. I know mother enjoyed meeting our friends and the friendly northern hospitality.

Great excitement was prevalent in the community as most of the children were going on the next train to Edmonton. They were to join other school children to see Queen Elizabeth and King George VI. The Royal couple were visiting that northern Alberta city during their royal tour. It was the first time for most of these children to see large buildings, shopping areas, street cars, and so many things people in the cities took for granted.

With the spring also came the inspection of the detachment. This included everything from the stamps on hand to the living quarters. Requests were made for a steel cell to replace the wooden one that was there. As well, we asked for permission and material to change the canoe to a square-ender. The motor mount would be on the back instead of the side.

While the inspection was still under way, word arrived that a local man was missing. There was concern that he was desperate and may have

King George and Queen Elizabeth's visit to Edmonton, 1939

taken his life after viciously attacking his younger brother. The younger brother managed to escape, and make it to the detachment to report the incident. My husband took off for a long day of searching the muskeg, coming back in the evening for more help. He arrived home to find that he also had me to worry about. I was in the early stages of labour, so he walked me to the hospital.

Tommy went with an expert Indian guide who could follow the movements of any moving creature through the bush. Towards morning they found the poor chap where he had hung himself in a tree. He had used his shirt as a rope. On this case the Indian guide had led my husband seven miles through hard to navigate muskeg country. This incident made us realize very quickly the natural abilities of those early Indians. Also towards morning, a little daughter was born. My husband has often mentioned the three anxious times that ended at once. The inspection was over, the search for the missing man, although tragic, and a new little member to our family had arrived safely.

Medicine has really advanced since 1939 in many fields, and one of these being maternity cases. As I look back I wonder from where the treatment of those days derived.

Our early ancestors had their babies, often with great difficulty. They were soon up and about as I am sure nature meant us to be. However when our first baby arrived, I was given the best of care. I had a fine doctor, and his staff at the new eight room Catholic hospital that was recently built in Fort McMurray. Most of the white women went to Edmonton in those days to have their babies, but we had true northern babies. I was well cared for and I did nothing for myself. I wasn't even allowed out of bed for a week. The day I was to go home was the fourteenth day after the baby's birth. I had a set back possibly due to inactivity and weakness, so spent another four days propped up in bed. When I finally could go home, I was very weak. I was, oh so grateful to have the help of a kind mother-in-law, who could stay for a couple more days. I am sure when she made the trip north for that special occasion, she didn't think that she would be away from her busy home in Edmonton for so long. I so often think about that first stay in hospital and realize that today new mothers hardly have time to rest before going home. In a few short days they become equipped to take on the role of a new mother. They are not weak from spending so long in their beds.

Our second summer in the north was equally beautiful and busy, it was especially so with our little girl. Everyone seemed to love her, the natives wanted to see the "Schmagonis's" little blonde papoose. (Schmagonis means police officer) They would stop us on the street to peek into the wicker buggy we had inherited. Everyone loved her but Puggy. From the very day we arrived home with that little bundle, he showed a decided dislike for the new intruder. We tried everything possible to let him know he was still special, but he never liked Betty. As time went on and she started to creep he kept his distance. He would growl viciously if she neared his special blanket under the kitchen stove.

I recall one day while taking the baby for a walk with Puggy on a leash, a friend stopped us to take a peek at the sleeping baby. Before either of us could stop him, Puggy, jumped into the buggy. The reason was not to protect the little charge but to be the one admired. This he made very clear!

That summer, our loved doctor, his wife, and family moved from Fort McMurray for health reasons. Until that next fall, we were without a doctor. Many a native came to see Tommy with some problem or another. With the help of the local druggist the best care possible was given to these people. We were thankful there were not any real serious cases before the new doctor arrived in the fall.

One day that same summer, a radio announcer told a shocked world that we were at war. The next train south took all of our young men away to train for the services. My husband wanted to join up at that time. He remained as did so many others who where needed to protect the home front. Our druggist's eldest son, a fine lad who had been our paper boy was one who went. I remember him as he came to our house to collect money to pay for the paper. He would call in the door and say, "Mrs. Paull do you have any chocolate cake today?" Incidentally, I always made a chocolate cake the same day that he collected money for the paper.

This lad went in to the air force and returned after training as an officer. He came home to say good-bye. We never saw him again as he gave his life in the early years of the war.

For some the war meant jobs after years of unemployment. Our neighbour had a hard winter trying without result to establish a good life. He decided to enlist in the navy, which developed into a full satisfying engineering career. The little house they had built next door seemed so empty. I'm sure they still have memories of their first home, hardships endured, and of the friendship we still hold so dear.

The war years found everyone doing everything possible to help. Our local I.O.D.E. chapter gained recognition for the war bonds sold, and the quantity of socks, scarves, and sweaters sent by such a small group. We sent with them our prayers for safety and hopes that our efforts gave comfort to some of those serving to save our freedom.

David Hill leaving Fort McMurray to go overseas, 1944

Baby Betty and Puggy

Paull family in Fort McMurray, 1941

Betty in Fort McMurray, 1941

Paull family in Fort McMurray with family house in background

Early Hill drugstore — Fort McMurray

LEARNING TO COPE

Managing on a limited quantity of water that we had either to haul a distance or buy by the barrel, or melt snow in the winter, was always a problem. I was accustomed to an unlimited amount in my mountain home town.

Bathing was a problem, with the baby having the luxury of fresh water. Then I washed the diapers and baby clothes in the bath water after the bath. Fresh water was used for rinsing, then to wash the kitchen floor, so every drop was well used. Bath night was usually only once or twice a week. I heated water for the bath on the stove. When it was the right temperature I poured it into the round wash tub. We had our baths on the kitchen floor, in front of the oven of our wood and coal stove.

Everyone had a turn from the little one first, and with my poor husband usually getting the last well used water. Once while climbing in for his turn, he found the baby's shoe laces floating in the water. He good-naturedly complained to our friends that his turn came after the washing was done. He probably felt fortunate that his turn proceeded that of our bull dog, Puggy, who loved his bath. He was restrained from joining each one as they had a turn.

Baby food in cans was unheard of. Babies not raised on natural milk were usually given bottles of milk from a mixture of water and powdered Klim. This was usually a real problem to get smooth milk that wouldn't clog the nipples. Other than milk, babies were fed little else in the early months until porridge and mashed canned vegetables were added gradually. Maybe our little ones should have had solid foods earlier, but they seemed to grow up sturdy and healthy.

Night feedings during the cold northern nights were trying times. Stoves were well banked at bedtime and often replenished during the night. Usually when the thermometer dipped to the minus forty or fifty degrees fahrenheit, the house would be bitter cold by six in the morning. The baby would awake for a feeding. While the baby cried impatiently, a fire was built. Soon the room would be warm and the water heated from the water pail. (Usually, it would be quite stiff by this time.) These duties usually fell to me as we figured there wasn't much use of both of us getting up. Everything was waiting in readiness so it wasn't much trouble. One such morning as warmth was chasing the chill out of the kitchen, a loud banging was heard on the office door. Although it was around six in the morning, it was still pitch dark outside. When I opened the door a more frozen than alive Indian, fell in on the floor.

I called Tommy, who was all ready on his way at the sound of the commotion. Together we helped the poor soul to a chair. Icicles were hanging from his eyes, nose, and mouth, he looked like a hugh snow man. After cups of hot fluid and food, we found him to be a nearly blind man from the Janvier Indian reserve at Cheeham. He had walked many miles along the railway in the bitter cold to get relief supplies. How he managed to complete his journey in that bitter cold weather, with so little eye sight is beyond me! This man's name was Pierre Cougan. He lived to return to his home with his rations, but our lives would cross again in later years.

One cold fall day, Tommy wanted to know if I'd like to go to Edmonton. What excitement! This would be the first trip out of the north since we were first transferred. A chance to visit with family and friends. However, there was a catch. For the first time I was to be a matron for a female mental patient coming from farther north in route to Edmonton for treatment. There was an added excitement. The escort and matron from Fort Chipewyan was to be no other than the sergeant and his wife, Tommy had served with before. Tommy and the sergeant had built a lasting friendship. This was very evident by the warm welcome given to them by Tommy the day they arrived at the McMurray office. I recall when I first met them as one of the most embarrassing moments ever. I went to the office door and there stood two women, both dark skinned. The police officer's wife was of Spanish background and the patient was of Indian heritage. They were both nicely dressed and in fur jackets. In the moments before the introductions were made I didn't know which was the police officer's wife and which was the patient. There I stood with my mouth wide open, and I wonder to this day how much my uncertainty showed.

The escort trip was a tiring but uneventful trip. The patient although very confused, was not in any way violent. As long as she was comfortable she was not a problem. Tommy and I took turns staying with her, although I attended to her needs. Seeing to the care of the patient plus keeping an eye on the baby kept me very busy. The baby proved to be a very good traveller. She enjoyed the rough train ride over the muskeg country far better than the rest of us. By the time the two days and one night trip ended and we had the patient admitted to the hospital, we were very tired. We were in anticipation over being able to stay in Edmonton for the next couple of days until the train trip back.

Upon our arrival, I received the sad news that my grandfather had passed away. Suddenly, I found myself and the baby on our way to Banff to attend the funeral. This was a great financial burden on us as we had not planned for this extra trip, when we left Fort McMurray. As I thought about it, I remembered that early in our marriage we found where there was the will, there was a way. Tommy returned to Fort McMurray on the next train from Edmonton. After a few days of visiting in Banff with family and friends, I returned to Edmonton for a couple more days of visiting. I then returned to my northern home the following week.

I wasn't looking forward to travelling on the train, alone with the baby. We hadn't travelled far when I realized there were several people from Fort McMurray travelling on the same train. Visiting with them helped pass the time on this lengthy journey. Betty was again a good traveller. After she went to bed, I passed several hours playing bridge. My bridge partners included the lady hotel manager in Fort McMurray, the Catholic priest, and the new doctor who was of Jewish decent. If the game lacked the touch of experienced players, no one noticed.

There was lots of fun and good-natured kidding handed out by all of us. Different religious beliefs, races, and walks of life were of little importance among the northern people. The concern for each other seemed to over shadow any differences we might have had. I remember the kidding of the Catholic priest as he coaxed the Jewish doctor to have bacon and eggs the following morning. However, it was agreed that the doctor would eat pork at the priest's wedding. The two became the closest of friends as they ministered together in their own field in that northern community.

We met so many interesting people during our stay in Fort McMurray. People on various missions as well as police personnel coming and going on escort or postings to different parts of the north. They often would have a few hours or sometimes days to put in while awaiting transportation.

We always tried to make our home a pleasant spot for our guests to visit. Puggy's tricks became well known and several came to see this clever little dog.

I recall some of the northern pilots, looking forward to a fresh Spanish onion sandwich with onions from the garden. For those who haven't tried them yet, they really are very good.

Another time I recall a visit from a member who had been in the far north for a bit too long and was on his way south. He was quite a worry to my husband as he had one thing on his mind and that was to have his fill of beer. We thought the best way to keep him off the street was to keep him at the house. I can't say that it was without its humorous moments.

After a couple of hours and several bottles of beer, our guest decided that he needed to have a drinking partner. He started to share his drinks with Puggy. They began taking turns drinking from the same bottle. Before long Puggy was staggering, in a comical way. When Puggy tried to lay on his pillow he would miss it. Fortunately Puggy's drinking partner fared better than him. After many cups of coffee and good food, he was ready to carry on his journey south. Maybe he was able to drown some of his frustration and loneliness.

Another experience made us very grateful that the old wooden cell was replaced by a steel cell. It had a solid steel floor, top, two latticed sides, and a front where the door was. The cell was at the end of the office with a five-foot passage between the kitchen wall and the door of the cell.

One day a call came for Tommy to go for a fellow, well- liquored up and on a rampage in the town. He proved to be a big, hard-rock miner in from the wilderness and after a few drinks had turned wild. How Tommy had ever managed to bring him from town and finally into the cell, fighting and yelling all the way, I will never know. Without help he was unable to remove his boots and clothing, hoping that after a cooling down period he'd be rational and easier to handle. Within a short period our guest was sound asleep and his snores were heard in the living quarters. As was the usual procedure when prisoners were in the cell overnight, Tommy went to get a night guard. Tommy was away for a short time, when our man awoke, sick, and in a rage. Lying on his back on the floor, he started to kick the door with his hobnail boots. This shook the whole house, sending dishes flying out of cupboards and landing all over the kitchen floor. I was very frightened, but went down into the office hoping that when he heard a women's voice he might settle down. However, that wasn't the case. I heard a lot of words that I hadn't heard before or since as he looked out at me, all the while kicking at the door. I could see the hole where the pad lock was, actually coming out of the steel. He continued kicking and moved the entire cell inches from the wall. Finally in desperation I got a revolver and decided if he broke out of the cell he wouldn't get into the house. By now the baby woke and cried with fright. I don't really know what I would have done if I actually had to defend myself that night. This was the way my husband and night guard found us. I was glad to turn the situation over to trained hands. The next day the chap, well sobered by then wanted to apologize to me after he was informed of how he had behaved. I was grateful that I didn't have to face him as I was still burning from the tongue lashing I had received the evening before.

There was a variety of cases that Tommy was called on but one of the saddest cases for me involved four little children. Apparently each child had a different father and were living in a filthy, wretched home with no sanitation, little food and care. It was decided that for their welfare they would be moved to Edmonton, where they would receive proper care. I was again asked to go as Matron. I made dozens of sandwiches and cookies to take with us. We then started with our little charges ranging from four to twelve years of age, plus our ten-month-old daughter. I remember the tears and fears of those sad little people as they left, terrible as it was, the only security they had known. They were filthy dirty and the soles of their feet were like shoe leather with the dirt and callouses from going without shoes. Things were going much better by the time we arrived in Edmonton a couple of days later. After several good washes and full tummies, they were beginning to respond to kindness. They seemed prepared for the new experiences and sights they would see for the first time in the city and hopefully a better life. It had been a very long and hard trip both emotionally and physically. The rainbow at the end for us was a few days with family and friends before returning on the next train north.

Once again my return to Fort McMurray was delayed. Break-up in the north was just over, and a raging forest fire had broken out threatening the community of Fort McMurray. We decided that I would stay in Edmonton with the baby until the danger was over. Tommy returned immediately because his help was needed.

This brings to mind some special friends whom we had the opportunity to meet. Mr and Mrs. Ransom, who were at Gordon Lake on a Ducks Unlimited Project. One day in the fall a pilot friend of ours invited us to fly with him and some friends. We flew the fifty miles to visit this fine couple. They were isolated at this spot except by air. It was my first time in an airplane so was a thrill to go on the trip. The real thrill was meeting this wonderful couple.

Marguerite was a nursing graduate from Walla Walla, Washington and had gone to be with her husband at this isolated spot. They often didn't see people for months and I was the first white woman Marguerite had talked to for six months.

Their home was comfortable, but every bit of the furniture was handmade from material found in the area. They had stores of canned goods, which had been flown in; otherwise they lived off the land, with fish, meat, and fruit. We had all taken food and had a wonderful day. As we left and flew off into the sunset, we looked down and standing there watching was Guy and Marguerite waving good-bye. On the way home, we marvelled at the way they were managing.

The following spring a near tragedy occurred at Gordon Lake. Guy had been fishing and a jack fish bit his hand. This bite resulted in a bad case of blood poisoning. His temperature raged, and he became unconscious. Marguerite, a nurse, did all she could with her limited amount of drugs on hand. Although she kept the infection under control for awhile, Guy was sinking lower each day. She kept trying to send S.O.S messages on the wireless, but because she was inexperienced with that part of the equipment, she couldn't make a connection. The day came when the last of the drugs had been given. Marguerite was beginning to wonder just what she would do when the end came. That same day a northern pilot was flying over the area. The pilot got in contact with the McMurray signal office to ask if there were any messages for the Ransoms. There had been some concern because of the lack of communication from the Ramsons. The people at the signal office asked the pilot to land and check on their welfare.

When he landed at the end of the ramp he was met by an almost hysterical Marguerite. They managed to get Guy on the plane and soon had him in Fort McMurray hospital. After weeks of care, he overcame the infection and regained his strength.

While I was in Edmonton, Guy and Marguerite stayed at our place in Fort McMurray, while Guy was recuperating.

The following week I returned from Edmonton to McMurray. I was relieved to hear that the spring rains had controlled the forest fire and that our community was safe. I was glad that our friends could find a haven in our home at the end of their nightmare.

The signal station at McMurray had a personnel of signal corp members and their families. The Major and his wife had received a refrigerator in their furnished home. It was of great interest to everyone in the community, the first we ever knew about any such convenience device. Someone asked me if I had gone over to see this machine that kept things cold in the hottest summer weather and even made ice. I laugh now, we the owners of not only a fridge but a deep freeze as well. I wouldn't let myself be tempted to go and see it. I think that maybe I felt a bit envious of something I was sure we would never own. However, it was a great step forward for those who could afford one. For those who would follow us, they were an asset if nothing more than to have fresh meat in the summer months.

With our small wages we seldom had more than a few cents change in our pockets for odd treats. Tommy did enjoy cigarettes and although he changed to smoking home made ones it still would cost us about three dollars a month. I was the chief cigarette maker and one day we decided I should have an equal amount to spend on a luxury.

Each month I kept an equal amount to put away for the longed for gift, a movie camera to give Tommy for Christmas. Everyone it seemed, had a movie camera.

With Tommy's new camera we joined in the fun, everything that moved seemed to have a camera aimed at it. What fun we had when the films would come in on the train! We would join with friends for a projection party. We had pictures of Puggy's tricks, happy picnics on the summer sand bars along the Clearwater River, and many dinner parties. Again it seemed as though we were always eating!

With very limited good radio programs and long before the invention of television, these home movie parties were real highlights during our northern years.

Late summer of our second year Tommy had a trip to Chard — mile 213 on the Northern Alberta Railway. We decided that our small daughter, Betty and I would go along and visit Mr. and Mrs. Raboud and their family. They lived in Chard and ran the trading post. Our trip on the railway was an experience in itself as we travelled in the caboose on the south bound freight train. As I looked back over the rails we had just travelled, I saw the roller coaster appearance as the rails rose and fell on the muskeg rail bed. Then I could well understand why the trip was so rough. Betty and I had the one comfortable chair in the car and on one occasion shot the length of the car, luckily not upsetting. It really took balance to stay on one's feet, and when our stop approached we were happy to disembark.

Mr. Raboud met us at the station with a wagon and team of horses, we started on another new experience. We had to ford the Christina River which looked treacherous to me but was actually nothing compared to what it would have been like earlier in the year. In the spring, the river was swollen with melting snow. Now, the fall colors were in evidence and the ten mile trip through the wooded trail was beautiful with colored foliage. It was something to see the saskatoons and chokecherries hanging in profusion filling the air with tantalizing perfume. The deer could be seen occasionally watching as we passed, ever ready to make a hasty retreat. I so enjoyed that trip.

The Raboud family consisted of six members; mother, father, two girls, and two boys. With the exception of a few items which they bought, they existed entirely off the land.

The meal that the Rabouds served to us that night consisted of roasted meat, delicious home grown vegetables, and freshly baked bread.

This lovely meal was preceded by the best home made beer I have ever tasted. I am not a beer drinker, but did enjoy what they had made so much. I even copied down the recipe so I could make some. Incidentally, our first effort was a dismal failure. Beer was something we never did learn to make successfully.

These fine people seldom had company and there was never any royalty treated with finer hospitality than what we had there.

They had a pet deer that they called Pedoo. Pedoo followed everyone around like a dog. We took movies of our little year-old daughter, following behind the deer hanging onto it's little flag tail. The little fellow would come to the door and knock at feeding time. The deer, like other pets, was often allowed to wander through the house.

Betty, Dorothy, and Tommy at Rabouds — Pet deer in background, 1940

"Pedoo", pet deer at Raboud's home

When it came time for us to leave this home, we had great admiration for our new friends. They were succeeding at living many miles from civilization, and enjoying it immensely. We treasured the pictures taken of this family outside their home hewn out of logs. It was beautifully finished both inside and out.

Our return trip to the rail road siding was as pleasant returning as going. We were fortunate enough to be in time to board the weekly passenger train en route to Waterways for a more comfortable trip home.

Although, I was mindful of the trips my husband made to the same area under much different circumstances. I recall one trip when Tommy set out with a rented dog team belonging to Lee Godwin.

It took three days to make the fifty to sixty mile trip from Fort McMurray to Rabouds. He had many stops to make on the way which almost ended in tragedy. As they were going through the gate into the Rabouds yard the dogs spied a tame deer. Immediately, the dog team broke into a frenzy trying to get at the deer. Tommy was thrown from the dog sleigh and landed against the fence, which broke his collar bone on impact. In much pain he called upon every effort to control the dogs.

For the next couple of days, Tommy was barely able to move, but it seems trouble seldom comes singly. This was no exception. At the little trading post, Mr. Raboud had an Indian interested in buying a .22 rifle. The fellow wanted to purchase it for hunting muskrats. Mr. Raboud went with the Indian and demonstrated the gun, then returned to the store where there were other Indians waiting to shop. While the Indian was trying to decide whether to buy the gun or not, he pumped it one more time, thinking it was empty and pulled the trigger.

The bullet hit Mr. Raboud in the instep of his foot. After a long night of keeping the foot in ice packs, it became clear that word must be sent to Edmonton. They needed an emergency plane to come to take Mr. Raboud to the Edmonton hospital.

Fort McMurray was the closest place to send a message. They decided that the plane would circle the area twice and then land on a lake, about three miles away. They would have to take Mr. Raboud there by dog team and sleigh.

The next morning Tommy started with the dogs well rested and ready to go on a most unforgettable trip. Tommy with a broken collar bone, was aching and in great pain. That morning it seemed like the dogs wanted to chase every rabbit or small animal that moved. Upon arrival at Fort McMurray, Tommy sent a message through the signal corp to Edmonton. A mercy plane was dispatched to pick up the wounded trader.

Fortunately, the doctor was able to remove the bullet successfully. After a prolonged stay in the hospital, Mr. Reboud was able to return to the north. Mr. Reboud ran the store in the same area for many years.

Incidentally, Tommy required medical treatment but thoughts for himself were second to his concern for his injured friend.

One day word reached the office that survivors of an aircraft had made their way out to report a plane crash. Tommy, who took charge of a search and rescue team, left for the reported area. The snow was deep in the bush and the travelling was rough. When the search party reached the area of the downed plane, it was a scene of tragedy, suffering, and bravery. The Canadian Airway Junker monoplane with eight on board, had engine failure as the plane had reached an altitude of 1200 feet. It had descended quickly, sheering tree tops off for one hundred and fifty feet before it came to a halt. With a crippled wing it plunged to the ground. A broken tree stump crashed through the fuselage, killing two of the passengers and seriously injuring others. It was fortunate that two of the passengers were able to walk out and report the crash. Although the pilot was injured, he comforted and took care of the remaining injured passengers.

A few days later several of us hiked to the accident sight. It would have been very difficult to spot, as it was in a heavily treed area and covered by freshly fallen snow. It is understandable why so many accidents are so difficult to locate. Especially in the winter months when snow has freshly fallen.

The tragedy shook our little community, and I was so glad that it was the only plane crash during our stay there. We were all so grateful that although two people were killed, the rest were rescued successfully. The injured passengers were brought back to Fort McMurray for treatment.

Christmas that year, with an active year and a half old daughter, was such fun. With friends, we went into the woods on the Sunday before Christmas on a Christmas tree hunt. We had a few tree decorations that we kept from other years. We added to these by threading popcorn and making paper chains. Our tree was beautiful! That Christmas all our friends must have given Betty a doll. Under the tree on Christmas morning were seven little rubber dolls of all descriptions: some white, one black one, and two little brown dolls. We went to bed that night visualizing the happy look that would be on our little one's face the following morning. We found out that we had overlooked one small item.. Puggy, although well house trained had never had the pleasure of having a tree in the front room before. Fortunately the dolls missed his misdemeanour.

Christmas morning was certainly all we had imagined, and our camera was busy as we took pictures of all the festivities. Betty had the difficult choice as to which doll would get the first ride in the red sleigh that Santa had brought. Finally, with a lot of careful thought the black doll was the lucky one. This was definitely a treasured Christmas. It was one of the very few Christmas's that Tommy wasn't called out to some tragedy or other.

A new member, our little son Ron, joined the Paull family on the first day of Spring that year. We were fortunate to have a fine girl from Edmonton, who was visiting in the area, stay and look after Betty while I was in the hospital. The day we brought our little bundle home was a happy day for all but for Puggy. That same little dog who had resented Betty, took one look, walked out of the house, out of the yard, and across the settlement. He went directly to a childless home where he had stayed the few times when we had been away. Poor little dog never did want to live with us after that.

Puggy went to live in Edmonton with the young girl who had stayed with Betty while I was in hospital. Hopefully, he was happier there. I hope he added the same amount of joy to her life that he had given to us.

One of our local half breed girls from a good home often came over to take Betty for buggy rides. Betty loved to go off with Madeleine, and after a few instructions like; don't take her into anyone's home or out of the buggy, they were off.

One day Madeleine didn't return at the usual time and we became quite worried. Tommy looked all over the town but no one had seen either of the girls. When seven o'clock came, we were beyond worry. It was two hours past the time they were usually back. Finally, we saw Madeleine pushing a happy little girl home. Madeleine was surprised to find us so distressed, as she felt she had given Betty a real treat. Betty had been taken in her buggy, in a canoe with friends of Madeleine's. Heaven knows, which friends, for a ride down the mighty Athabasca River. Her intentions were good. She told us that she hadn't taken Betty out of the buggy or into any one's home. Then we knew that she meant well.

We realized quite quickly that the thinking of a northern girl was much different from our own. A few more restrictions and instructions were to be imposed before Betty was given into her charge again.

After several attacks of an extremely sore throat, illness seemed to be plaguing Betty. With few drugs to combat the infection, the doctor advised us that her tonsils be removed. Although she was only two years old at the time, this was the action taken. It wasn't long before there was a noticeable improvement in her heath.

I feel all would have been well if it weren't for a whooping cough epidemic that had hit the town. About a month after her operation, not yet very strong, Betty came down with this disease. That summer was a nightmare of sick babies! Betty came down with whooping cough, and Ron at five months of age as well. I'm sure many can remember the frightening experience of children having that dreaded disease before the days of immunization. When Betty coughed, the baby would seem to have a spasm and turn blue as he fought for his breath. For nights on end, Tommy and I took turns sitting up with the children. We would have one hand resting on the crib and the other on the buggy, alert to either of their needs. Past summer trips were just a pleasant memory as we combatted that dreadful childhood disease. It lasted most of the summer and into the fall.

One day in early September, we received word that a woman from the Janvier Indian Reserve had died under strange circumstances. Our friends the Rabouds lived on this reserve and had their trading post there.

The doctor from McMurray, (who was also the coroner), and Tommy left for Janvier. They first sent messages requesting for extra help from Edmonton. An incident such as this caused a real stir amongst the town's people in our usual quiet little town. The doctor's new wife, spent most of the time at our place when the men were away. She was very uneasy about her husband's unusual change of work.

With the usual flow of people who came to the door on various missions, plus two sick children of our own, I was plenty busy. It didn't take long for me to realize that this was just the start of several nerve racking days.

Tommy found out that the woman in Janvier had been killed in a very vicious manner, possibly with the blow from an axe. This woman was the wife of Pierre Cougan. Pierre was the near blind Indian who had fallen into our office near frozen, one cold winter day the previous winter. Pierre was the murder suspect. He was brought back to McMurray, and placed in the cell. I was glad that the wooden cell had been replaced by a steel cell. Especially now that we had a murder suspect under our roof. The body of Cougan's wife was brought back as well. The body was placed in the shed, waiting for a post mortem. By this time the body was starting to decompose. Along with Pierre Cougan and the body of his wife, were many witnesses. Of course, these Indian witnesses brought their families with them and set up camp in our yard.

It was a bit scary for a young officer to conduct the investigation and decide alone, what should be done. The arrival of Sergeant Broadrib from Edmonton was a great support.

The next few days our place was anything but quiet and pleasant. Fortunately for me the sergeant was a family man and very fond of children. Although that meant another person for meals, along with having to feed the Indian in the cell, the sergeant was much more helpful than troublesome.

The Indian witnesses going in and out of the office filled the house with the odour of buckskin and herbs. Although, worse was the odour of the decaying body that seeped into our house from the shed. The mounties assisted the doctor because there were no other qualified persons to help. It was a grim scene to see the doctor and the Mounties going back and forth from the office to the shed to perform the postmortem on the body. This was to try and determine the cause of death. They determined that the cause of death was by a severe blow to the head. As well as loss of blood from cuts that could not have been self inflicted. It was a great relief when the body was removed for burial. Pierre Cougan was flown to Edmonton. This was a very difficult investigation, covering miles of muskeg wilderness and interviewing native people, which had to be accomplished through an interpreter. During the next few weeks I saw very little of my husband.

Then a young constable arrived to look after the problems in McMurray while Tommy and the other mountie were away. It was very comforting to have someone in the house, as he occupied the little room off the office.

It was also a relief that the children were overcoming their coughs, but I still had problems with the baby. As soon as he had consumed a bottle of milk, he'd have a bad time, which usually resulted in him up chucking it all. An old northern nurse came to my rescue and suggested that I take away the milk and give him barley water and fruit juice. Can you imagine what we went through as we introduced this little fellow, to barley water. During those next few days he let us know of his disapproval. The barley water seemed to do the trick and the nightmare was a thing of the past.

The case of Pierre Cougan came before the courts in Edmonton nearly a month after the murder. It was necessary to try to have the trial before the Indians started to scatter on their winter work of trap lines.

This gave very little time for investigation. It must have been very difficult, because it entailed covering miles and miles of country. The Indians that were being interviewed could not understand the reasons behind all the questions. In their own minds they were sure and they thought the police were sure that Pierre had caused his wife's death.

When the train left for Edmonton on that October morning we were a motley crew. We had a woman prisoner so I was among them, as matron with two small children, travelling with Tommy. The Indian witnesses brought their families with them, because they couldn't be left at home alone. There were a couple of white witnesses along as well.

I still don't understand how Tommy stood up under all the strain. He had the work of making arrangements to get all of these people to Edmonton. He also arranged accommodation for these people while they were in Edmonton for the trial.

During the trial, there was a jury disagreement due to a woman hating judge. The presiding judge ordered a new trial that started immediately.

The court encouraged the Indians to tell all they knew about the case and to tell the truth. Even though the Indians and the police knew what the truth was, the Indians couldn't understand why they had to repeat their story for the man with the wig and the jury.

You can imagine the bewilderment of those native people in the strange surroundings, so sure of what happened in their own minds. The Indians just couldn't understand why they were asked so many silly questions.

The second trial, a repeat of the first, resulted in the second jury unable to reach an agreement. The result being that the court was going to set Pierre Cougan free. The poor natives, after co-operating with their evidence could not understand the white man's strange laws. When it was over the chief came to my husband and asked why Pierre might be going back to the reserve. Still not convinced that Pierre was innocent he said, " If Cougan come back, some day his canoe will tip in river." Indicating that they would take the law into their own hands, which would result in another investigation of possible murder. A plea was submitted to the crown prosecutor. He ruled that Pierre Cougan be kept in jail until the police had more time for further investigation. Another trial was set for the Spring.

Sergeant Broadrib continued to assist Tommy, and I'm sure he must have looked back on this case with mingled emotions. He loved the north with its beauty, and he liked to be a part of our family. However, his age and the city life had not prepared him for some of the rugged trips they had to make.

Sergeant Broadrib and Tommy on Cougan murder case, 1941, with Ranson's cabin in the background

Sergeant Broadrib and Tommy on Cougan murder case

I remember hearing about one trip they made to the reserve. They had been unable to notify Mr. Raboud of their arrival, who was usually there with transportation to the reserve. When they arrived at the train siding at Chard 213, they soon found out that the river was swollen by heavy rain. Equipped with the usual northern equipment, they chopped down trees and lashed them together with willows. They were able to make a raft big enough for two men and all of their travelling gear. Reports I heard made me glad that I was not there to witness the trip. They managed to pole the raft across swift moving river. The raft was carried a considerable distance down stream by the strong current before they were able to land the raft.

Arriving at Rabouds after a ten mile hike back they were glad to see their friends. Tommy couldn't believe how big Pedoo had grown, now sporting a fine pair of antlers. Pedoo was a real pet, and seldom left the yard. He wore a collar and bell to distinguish him from the hunted deer in the area. A while later however, we were sorry to hear that Pedoo had been shot. An Indian hunter hadn't realized that this deer was a pet of the traders.

Tommy, Sergeant Broadrib, Mr. and Mrs. Raboud with dog team, 1941

Another trip, that I recall hearing about was made by dog team in the early spring. The area was only accessible by dog team this time of year. Preparations were made and plenty of food taken for the time they expected to be away. Little did anyone know what trouble they would run into. One of the worst blizzards of that time blew in that spring, with severe cold temperatures, high winds, and blowing snow.

The sergeant, being the older man travelled much of the time in the sleigh, while Tommy ran or rode behind on the runners. When the storm blew up they were in the area of Gordon Lake. This was close to where Mr. and Mrs. Ransom were stationed with Ducks Unlimited. It was most fortunate that they could find their cabin in the storm and were most grateful for the shelter. Being nearly out of food, they managed to find enough among the supplies left in the cabin to survive. As soon as the weather cleared they left for home.

I was a very anxious wife when I finally welcomed the weary travellers home four days later than I expected them. The Sergeant's moccasins were blood soaked from the travelling on the sharp icy snow. He was full of praise for the endurance that Tommy had displayed during the long trip. Years of northern experience and being able to keep in good shape were possibly the reasons responsible for their safe return on that trip.

An incident that happened the last Christmas season that we were in Fort McMurray was without a doubt the most embarrassing incident ever. One good thing about it was that it has supplied us with many a good laugh. I attended the Anglican Church in Fort McMurray. Tom usually joined me on the Sunday of the month when the minister conducted an inter-denomination service for members from other churches. (The Anglican and Roman Catholic denominations had their own churches.) The church was not very large and the choir pews faced the centre, occupying the upper right side of the Church. The pews on the left of the church reached as far as the upper end of the choir pews.

One of our neighbours sang in the choir and her husband joined my husband and I for the Christmas service. When we arrived the small church was nearly full. The usher led us to the front pews on the left side of the church just opposite the choir.

The Christmas service was beautiful. We whole heatedly joined in the singing of our favourite carols. We listened intently to the Christmas scriptures.

During the announcements the minister announced there would be Holy Communion following the service. He also said that whether we were Anglican or not we were welcome to participate. We were discussing as to whether we would stay after or not, and missed the next announcement. The choir was to sing the first two verses of "Silent Night" and then the congregation would join in the remaining verses. The music started, up stood the choir, the minister and the three of us. In spite of glares from our friend's wife in the choir we sang the wonderful hymn with enthusiasm. During the second verse I happened to notice that the congregation behind us were seated. I passed this message on to the other two beside me, immediately realizing our mistake we sat down. As we sat down the rest of the congregation stood up to join the choir for the remaining verses. About this time the minister and the majority of the small choir, except for our friend, could hardly sing for laughing.

We felt badly that we had been the cause of the unexpected turn of events at that lovely Christmas service. We expect it has given many a laugh over that Christmas season and since.

As each season in the north had its own beauty it was hard to decide which season we loved the most. The winters were cold, with long nights and short daylight hours, but we enjoyed the outings to their fullest.

Bundled up in parkas, and mukluks, tramping out in the crisp snow are events that we have long remembered. Winter travel for the mounties often was done by rented dog team or occasionally by plane.

The spring and summer days were long with very little dark. It was possible to be able to read even at midnight without lights, so it was never really very dark. The flowers that grew in the northern gardens were as beautiful as flowers grown anywhere. During these months the mounties made their patrols by powered canoes; often we went along. We would stop occasionally at a sandbar for a picnic and a dip in the clear, summer warmed, unpolluted water.

The fall was also a beautiful time of the year, when the foliage took on the gorgeous hues of red, yellow and orange. The air was full of the perfume of ripened berries. I remember the northern lights of the fall and early winter. The sky would just dance and at times it would look to be on fire with the coloured Aurora Borealis. I found it hard to decide which season of the year we enjoyed the most. In spite of the trying times, we treasured those years spent in that fascinating part of the country.

Paull family leaving the north in route to Stettler, 1942

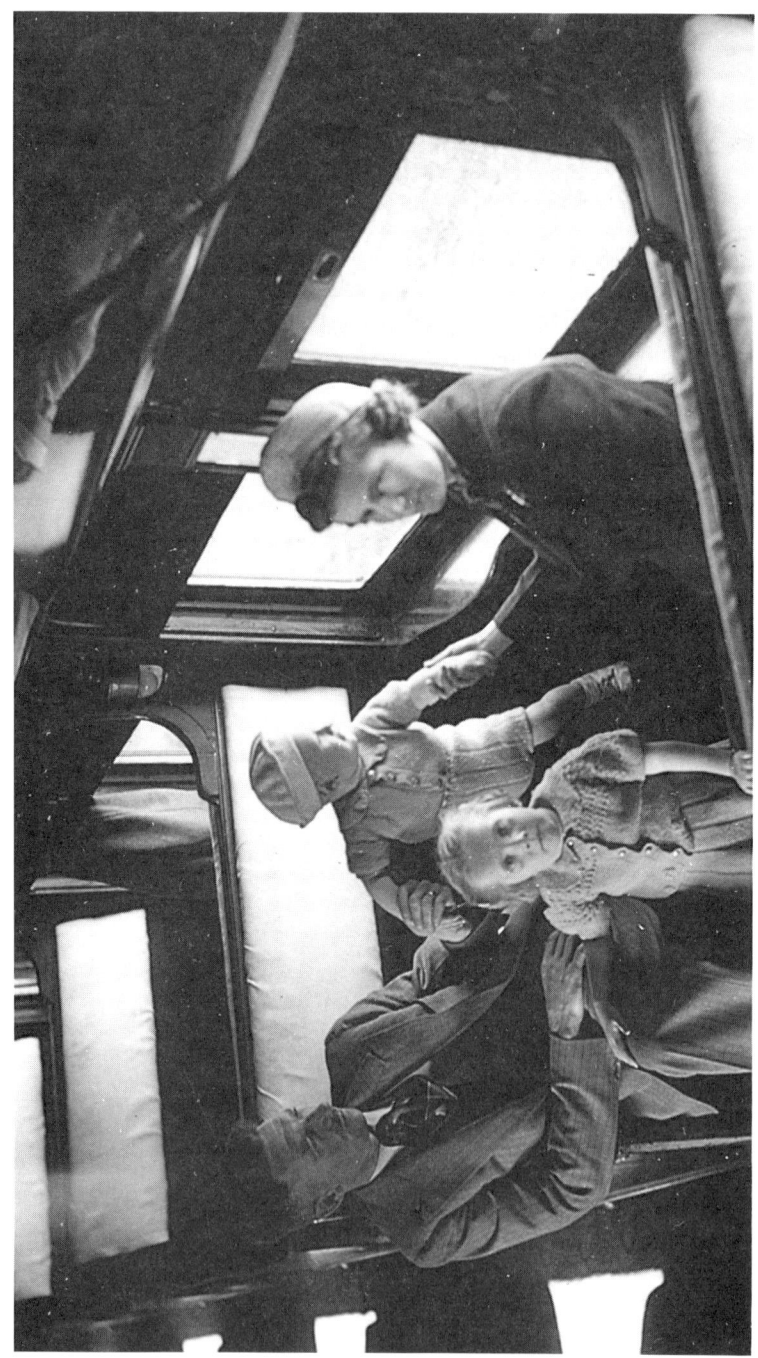

On N.A.R. (Northern Alberta Railroad) on way to Stettler, 1942

OUR NORTHERN YEARS END — NEW POSTING — STETTLER

As our fourth spring approached so did the news of our being transfered to Edmonton with the Criminal Investigation Branch. It was with mixed emotions that we started to pack and crate our furniture for the trip south. We combined our transfer with taking about thirty witnesses including their families to the final trial for Pierre Cougan. The trial took place in the spring of 1942. The evidence brought before the judge and jury resulted in a murder verdict. The court sentenced Pierre Cougan to life for the brutal murder of his nearly blind wife. A year less a day after the crime was committed and after three trials in Edmonton.

It was hard to say good-bye to our dear friends that we made during those four years in the north. Although, the anticipation of seeing family and friends in Edmonton plus the idea of having a few luxuries gave us much to look forward to.

Our last weekend in the north found us taking a hike to where the area was being cleared by bull dozers for the first landing strip. This would make plane landing possible even during breakup and freeze up times of the year. We weren't able to see the completion of this project. Somehow we knew that this would be the first real large step forward in promoting that community to the oil and tar sands boom area that it is today.

Just before leaving we were notified to ship our belongings to Stettler instead of Edmonton. In Stettler, Tommy would take charge of another detachment.

After a few days in Edmonton, we were driven to Stettler by the patrol sergeant, and what a trip! Our little ones, not being used to travelling by car, were car sick most of the way, we thought we would never get there.

We had understood that we would move into quarters vacated by the member that was transferred out. What a jolt we received when we finally arrived to find that they had lived in a one bedroom suite. The living accommodations were over a garage and impossible for a family of four to occupy. We stayed in a hotel for a couple of days while my husband attended to the office transfer and found accommodations. It seemed impossible to find a place to rent in town. Finally, we located and rented a big farm house on the outskirts of town.

My husband's office was upstairs in the court house. To our pleasure and surprise our dear friend and doctor who had delivered Betty in the Fort McMurray hospital was the health doctor. His offices were downstairs in the same building.

In McMurray our furniture seemed adequate in that small northern home but in this large roomed farm house nothing looked cosy. The grass had grown around the empty house, three or four feet high and the children had great fun hiding in it. One day while Ron, now age two, was hiding he ended up taking a nap. We had an anxious time until we found him, curled up, and fast asleep.

There seemed to be plenty to do to keep myself busy, but even so decided to dig a garden spot. The soil was rich and loamy. It wasn't long before we had a garden planted and we were looking forward to green vegetables.

We soon discovered that something else was watching our garden very closely. They especially enjoyed the pea and bean seeds that they found on top of the soil. Two gophers were taking control of the area and they sat up and scolded us soundly when we went near. I planted several times with the same result. One day I asked my husband to load the .22 rifle and I'd try to get rid of them. The next day when I saw the two trespassers, I aimed and shot a couple of times. I must have been dead serious as I managed to get both gophers. From that time on our garden had a good chance and did well.

My husband was busy that first summer. After having our home in the detachment for so long, I missed him being around. I found the days to be very long. The mile walk to town with the two little ones often took a good part of the afternoon. I enjoyed walking around looking at our new town. I was hoping to see some place in town to rent. As I looked, I often felt a lump in my throat. I realized then how much I missed our friends in the north.

Something that we learned the hard way was that Stettler's water was very soft with a high soda content. One evening I made a chicken stew and dumplings in one of my aluminium pots. The Provincial Licence officer who also worked in the courthouse, was an old timer of the community. We had decided to invite him over for dinner that evening. I thought the dinner was good and everyone seemed to enjoy it. One by one our family became deathly ill. We summoned a doctor. We were told, almost too late, that we couldn't use aluminium pots with Stettler water. I was worried about our elderly guest, Mr. Grey. He must have built up a resistance to it as he wasn't sick, for which we were very thankful. We had to replace all our cook ware with enamel and pyrex.

One day while on patrol, Tom found a three bedroom house in the neighbouring town of Big Valley. He found out that we could purchase it for $600.00. That seemed to be a high amount for us in those days but was the only way we could afford a home. We managed to buy a corner lot near the court house. A foundation was poured and the house moved on to it, although winter snow and cold weather had arrived before much could be done. It was a very exciting day when we moved from the farm to our Stettler home.

Part of one bedroom was made into a bathroom. With a good cleaning and some painting the house was made over to be a most comfortable home. As time went on the basement was finished. Next the front porch was enclosed with glass, and the back porch finished off.

The first glimpse that our new neighbour got of me was one of long lasting value, I'm afraid.

A plant that was given to me for Mother's day was in the process of being destroyed by aphids. Someone had told me that if I was to smoke it with cigarette smoke I could get rid of the aphids. Unable to find a cigarette, I settled for a cigar of Tom's. I decided there wasn't much difference between the two, and the cigar would work as well as the cigarette. I lit the cigar and put a tent over the plant that I had made from newspaper. I placed it all in the kitchen sink, then proceeded to puff and puff. A real cloud of smoke formed over the plant. Being a non-smoker my head began to reel. I emerged from the plant with the cigar held high over my head. I was gasping for every breath. Looking into our still uncurtained kitchen window was my new neighbour with a horrified look on her face.

It wasn't long, however, that our little ones got playing together and found that I had friendly neighbours.

With Tommy now closer to his work we quickly approached our first winter in Stettler, Alberta.

In off hours I believe the years we spent in Stettler were some of the happiest for Tommy. Although he worked twelve hour shifts, he found time to join good friends in curling, golfing, and hunting as the seasons allowed. We were introduced to bridge games during the winter evenings and we have many happy memories of the evenings spent with friends. I spent some time as the leader of the C.G.I.T. group. I found this to be a valuable experience as I worked with teenage girls. We seldom went any place where we couldn't take the children. When we needed a baby sitter it was generally one of the C.G.I.T. girls. They would come and as a rule were happy to receive the twenty-five or fifty cents for an evening's work. This was the regular amount paid in the early 1940's.

Promotion came to Tommy early in the transfer to Stettler. Although his work was in a large surrounding area he was not responsible for the town which had their own police. Many times however he was called to assist the town police. The county of Stettler had a large German population and this was war time. There were instances when an officer didn't want to be alone on patrol.

Ron (age 2) Betty (age 4)

Tommy, Ron and Betty in Stettler

C.G.I.T. group in Stettler, 1935

SICKNESS HITS OUR LITTLE GIRL

One day sickness hit our little Betty, who had been complaining of a sore hand at noon. An infection rampaged quickly through her little body and by night she was running a high temperature. The doctor diagnosed it as rheumatic fever. The next day she was in the hospital with her arm swollen twice the size it should have been. Her little body was racked with pain and fever. Two days later the doctor diagnosed it as osteomyelitis and by Saturday, she had surgery. Weeks of anxious watching and fervent prayers for her recovery passed before we could bring her home.

She was still a very sick little girl. After a short time we took Betty to Calgary, where she was admitted into the Crippled Children's Hospital. . She was under the care of Dr. C. Townsend the best orthopaedic doctor that we knew. We felt if anything could be done for our four-year-old daughter, it could be done here.

Life had to go on, but it went at a low ebb for us. We didn't have medical coverage in those days and the medical bills kept mounting up. With little money to pay the bills, there seemed to be nothing but hardship ahead. However, with prayers and our faith, plus the help of friends we met during those trying times we were able to make it through.

Our little son was growing up. Even though we missed Betty, and longed to have our little girl home with us, Ron brought us much joy and comfort.

One day Tommy was going hunting so Ron and I went along for the outing. We stopped at a slough where we spotted some ducks.. Ron armed with his wooden gun followed his Dad. Tommy raised his gun to shoot, closely followed by his wee son Ron. Just when Ron shouted, "BANG." Tommy shot and down came two ducks. In wild excitement our wee fellow said, "I got it, Dad, I got it." These were treasured memories for us.

One day a tearful young girl from a broken home called in at the police office to see Tommy. She had a beautiful well-bred golden Chow with her, a present from her father. Apparently, her step father refused to allow her to keep the dog. With a near broken heart she wanted to find a good home for "Chubby." To her relief Tommy said we would take him and give him a good home. This was how we acquired a new addition to our family. Once Chubby settled in to accept his new home and family he proved to be a wonderful pet. Few adults could touch him but ourselves. Our children and the neighbourhood children could do anything with him from riding him,

Stettler 1944. Wounded Betty and Ron

to dressing him up in their clothes. Chubby was a real joy to us all and a real protective pal for the children.

Friends were wonderful and looked after Ron one week each month while I went to Calgary where I stayed with relatives. Each day I'd walk to the hospital; spend all day with Betty and the little girls in her ward. The infection was anything but abated. Little could be done in those days for that dreaded disease. Sulpha was just a new drug, in those days, but it didn't seem to be curing this infection. Betty was well cared for and she was so happy. I sometimes felt that my visits interfered with the happy hospital routine of their lives as patients.

Tommy went to see her as often as he could. His visits had to be combined with work related duties that took him to Calgary. We felt this was the only way we could stay close to Betty.

On one of the visits I made, I found a Catholic Nun in the unit giving instructions to one of the little patients. Of course, she had a captive audience from the rest of the little girls. Betty could count beads like the rest of them. Another day while with them in the hospital something displeased Betty. She came out with a stream of naughty words. I told her that I didn't think they were nice words for a little girl to say. She replied, "Never mind Mommy. You can say anything you want as long as you cross yourself and say Holy Mary Mother of God." I was shocked! I found the protestants at that time hadn't managed to have guidance for their little patients. Soon after that incident they rectified the problem. Betty was able to return home for a short time, pending expected surgery to try and clear up the infection.

At this time we found out that we were going to add another little member to our family. How great it was to have our family all together when our second daughter was born in January, 1946.

Six weeks later in the middle of a very cold spell in February, we were transferred to Olds.

There was no easy way to move in those days but to get busy and pack ourselves. We moved all our things in the new detachment police van. It took several trips.

With a sick little girl, a little boy, and a new baby it was no easy task for us. With the doors opening and closing so much in the bitter cold weather the baby caught a bad cold.

Finally everything was packed but the baby was too sick to travel and Tommy had to go ahead while we stayed with friends. Because we couldn't go together, our move had to be done at our own expense. This added extra hardship for us, but such were the hard lives of those days. The sale of our house helped to ease some of the burden. This money helped us clear up some of our mounting medical debts. It was with mixed memories of happy and sad times that we left the lovely town of Stettler.

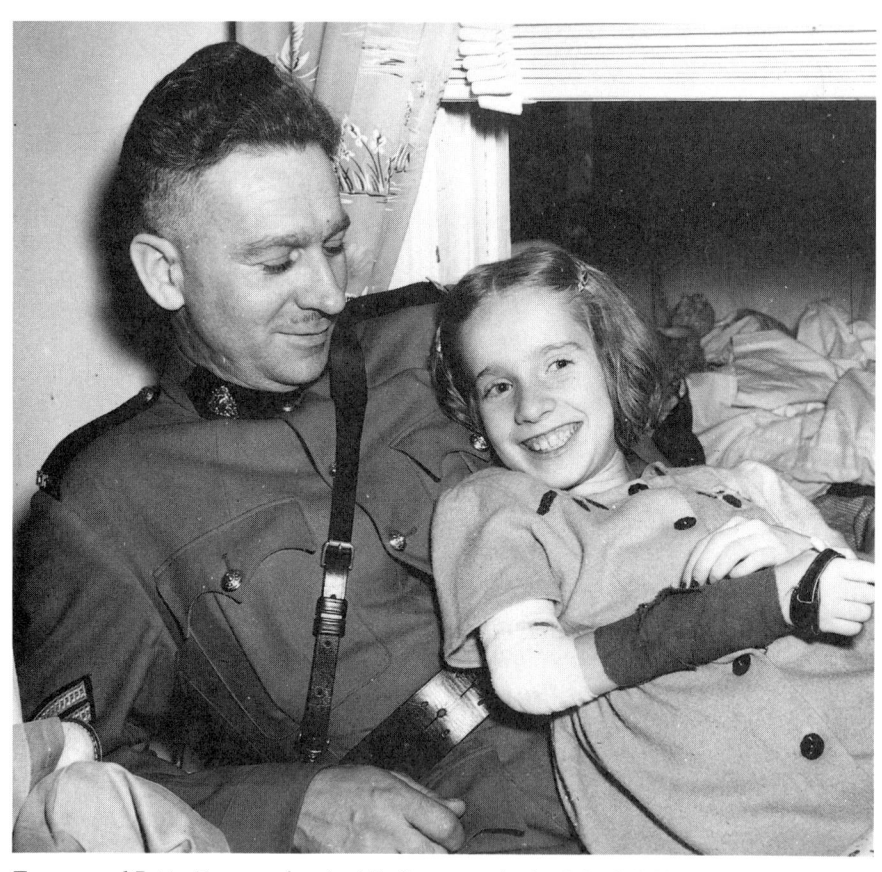

Tommy and Betty (6 years of age) while Betty was in the Crippled Children's hospital in Calgary

OUR NEXT MOVE — OLDS, ALBERTA

Our new home in Olds was in the detachment building. It had a good-sized office and a store room. We were happy there was not a cell in the building. We were right in the down town area and almost across from the hotel and beer parlour. However, it was a comfortable home with ample space for our family.

Water seemed to plague us where ever we went. Stettler water was so soft it riddled our aluminium pots. Olds water was so hard that about its only function was to flush the toilet and not always satisfactory either. The water came from wells, as water and sewer were still not a commodity of the town. Strangely, our well produced very hard water, while a deep well close by produced soft water. We hauled water from the soft water well.

Towards the end of our stay in Olds the wonderful invention of detergent came on the market. A sample of Dreft was left at the door, " Good in the hardest of water," it said on the package. I thought that nothing was good enough to help our water. What a wonderful surprise to find the water lathered and could be used for washing the clothes. I am sure the detergent was the conversation amongst most the house wives.

Olds was a two-man detachment and the junior officer was a fine chap whom Tommy enjoyed both at work and socially. They had the full policing of the town and district; seldom did they have time to be out of uniform. The detachment was really three strong as our dog Chubby went out on most of the patrols with either police officers. After the last rounds of the town were made, Chubby continued to check around to make sure everything was still all right. On more than one occasion Chubby, woke us by barking under our window. Tommy would jump out of bed, dress, and go running out to have a look. Chubby would lead him back to where some disturbance had aroused him. Strangers were not welcomed in the business area of the town at night. Chubby may have been a deterrent to night crime.

One year while we were on a holiday at Sylvan Lake, we took Chubby along to be with the children. While we were away there was a rash of breaking and entering reported. When we returned home, Constable Dick Jones informed us that next time we went on a holiday, we were to leave Chubby home. The lone member of the detachment needed his help to watch over the town. In spite of his attachment to the mounties he was still the family pet and a great playmate for the children.

Police cars in those days did not have radios in them and three broadcasts a day were recorded in the office. The men took the broadcast if they were home in time, otherwise, I would jot down the messages for them. Except for this small way to help and occasionally answering a knock on the office door, there was little call on a police officer's wife. Only a couple of times was I asked to serve as matron.

One time I was asked to help with a nine-year-old boy who had been picked up for robbery. He was very much in the need of cleaning up. My motherly instinct took over; after a good bath, he was dressed in freshly washed clothes. We gave him a good dinner then he had a chance to play with the children. He seemed such a good little boy, and I was sure he couldn't have been anyone who would have done anything wrong. Unfortunately, after he left, we found the money in the children's piggy-banks had also disappeared. Oh well, so much for my police efforts.

Baby Connie in Olds, 1946

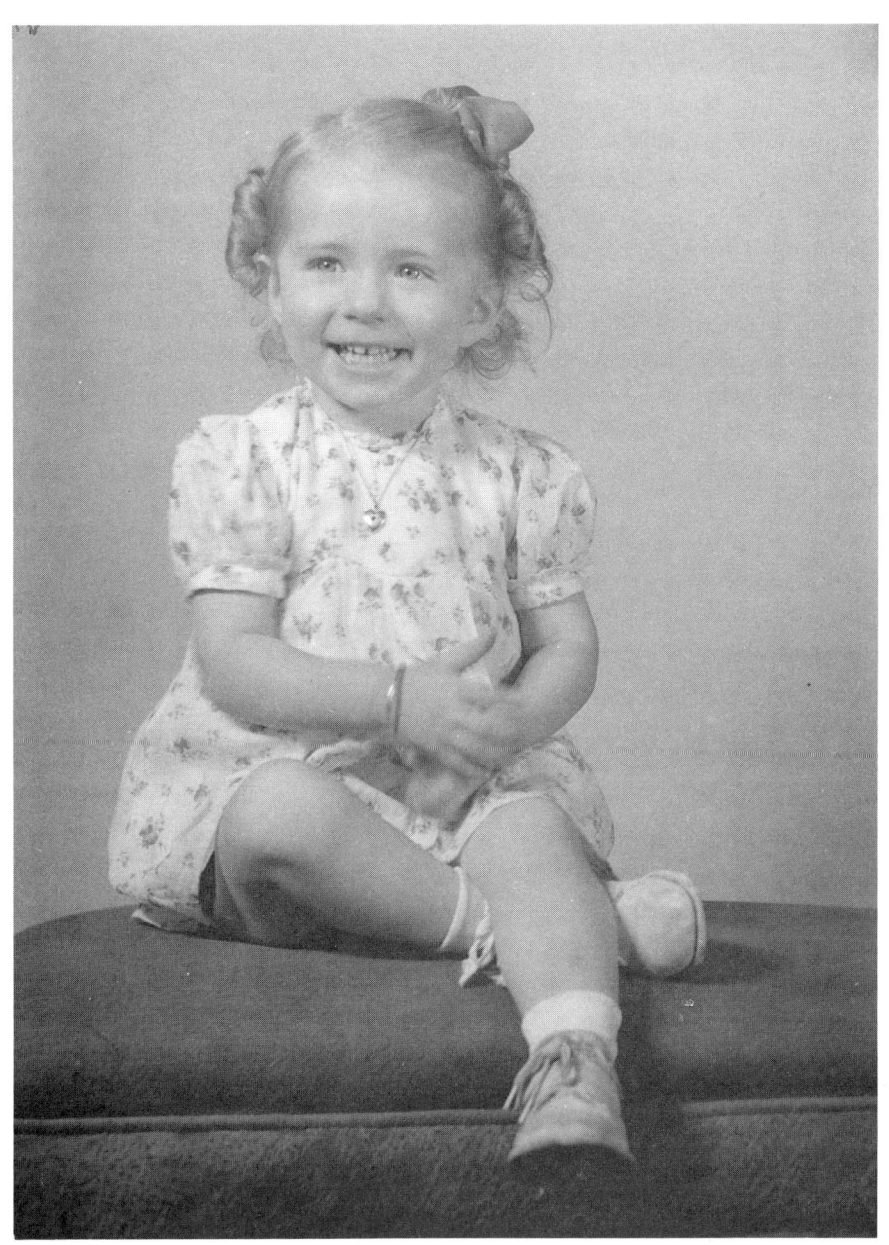
Connie at age 2, taken in Olds

Early in the spring our junior mountie Dick brought home his bride Isabel. We had many happy times together; when the men were away it was great to have the companionship of another member's wife's company. Our children also won a spot in their hearts, and Isabel and Dick became the god-parents of our baby Connie.

Betty was still going between the Calgary hospital and home. She was taking most of her early schooling by correspondence. She had a couple of operations to clear up the infections, but both had failed and her little arm had to be dressed each day, which was quite painful. A trip to the Mayo clinic in Rochester, Minnesota was high on our list of priorities. In Tommy's off hours and on holidays he spent all of his time building a trailer. By fall we were ready to take off for the appointment.

Betty, Connie, Ron and Chubby, 1947

We didn't have a car and in those post war years they were impossible to buy. We had a credit note from the sale of our car prior to going North. We were able to get a car by early September. Soon after that Tommy, Betty, and I started our trip to the Mayo clinic. Kind friends were so good to us and looked after the younger children while we were away. We had quite a trip and under happier circumstances would have been a nice holiday. There were very few trailers on the road those days, and I don't suppose we saw more than a dozen the entire trip. Having a trailer made it possible to take our daughter to where we hoped they could help her.

Following the trip to Rochester, Betty returned to hospital where after several more operations the infected area was cleared.

At long last Betty was able to return home. Now we were all looking forward to a brighter, healthier future.

We didn't have too many occasions to go out without the children, so it was seldom necessary to hire a baby sitter. However, we were fond of a neighbour's daughter and took her with us on holidays. We made arrangements with her to come on Saturday nights if she didn't have previous baby sitting jobs. In the evening she came to our house, we'd go out for a walk, a show, or on occasion out to visit.

One Saturday night we drove to a neighbouring detachment to help celebrate the promotion of one of its members. We just arrived only to receive word to return home quickly. Someone had broken into the police office. I can still recall the few minutes it took to make that speedy return home. Sure enough a fight had started across the road at the beer parlour ending by one escaping and running to the police office. Not being able to get in he broke through the window getting into the office and out the window of the store room. Of course, the noise attracted a crowd outside.

In the house was a near hysterical baby sitter who had left the sleeping children and escaped out the back door. This was the way we found things when we arrived home. No harm had come to the children, and our baby sitter had become an important person amongst her school chums.

Unknown to us at the time, we found out that all the attention wasn't necessarily good attention. She came from a fine home but with little frills or excitement. She began making plans as to how she might again gain recognition. A few Saturdays later while my husband was on duty, I attended a show with Dick and Isabel. When we returned home I went in the back door while my friends continued home. Upon entering, I called "Hello," but when there was no response, I went looking. When I saw the office door open, I was very surprised. The office was completely out of bounds to the baby sitters. When I looked into the office, I found the baby sitter lying inside the office door with a piece of wire around her neck. I hastily called the constable back who was still within hearing distance. We found out later that the entire deal was planned. Right up to making sure the piece of wire was the right size to fit around her neck just so. Her plan was foiled when I didn't go in the front door. She probably expected me to scream when I saw what was to look like an attack. After summoning her parents, their comment was, " Too many comics!" We summoned the doctor to make sure she was all right, then we sent her home. Early Monday morning before school that young lady received a good talking to from Tommy. She admitted that she had planned the entire thing hoping to gain more admiration from her school chums. It was a sad ending in our house as we were very fond of the girl. We couldn't afford to have her as our baby sitter, especially in a Government building. It was sad for our children who dearly loved their baby sitter.

Health problems plagued us once more. We no sooner felt that Betty's main problems were behind her, when our young son developed a limp. This required a trip to the specialist, Dr. Townsend in Calgary. (Who we credit for saving Betty's arm.) He gave us the bad news that Ron had a problem in his right leg that required complete rest in the children's hospital. It was a very sad time for us. Following the rest cure and required surgery we were assured that in time he should be all right.

We always looked forward to Christmas. It was so much fun while the family was little, full of excitement and happiness. In those days each officer received a Moiety cheque of $30.00 as a Christmas gift from a special fund. With wages still small the cheques were always appreciated. They brought the extras we enjoyed at that time of the year.

As I look back and think about our lives in Olds there were happy days, and we made friends who will always be special. We shared a yard with the mayor and his family. Fortunately for us they had a lawn mower. The R.C.M.P. didn't supply one and we weren't in a position to buy one. There certainly were no frills during those years. There weren't even police cars with signal lights, just the officer on night patrol with a flash light.

However, there were good times, and we saw progress in the town. About the time we were to move, the roads were all dug up as sewer and water pipes were installed. Although we weren't there to see them in operation, we knew the town of Olds would be a lovely place to live.

SOUTH TO HIGH RIVER

The time arrived for another move and this time to High River, a town south of Calgary. Such a move as that meant that we had to pack ourselves and move in the R.C.M.P. van. One of our loads went to High River. In High River the van picked up a load for the family that was moving to Calgary, followed by a load of the family moving to Olds. At the end of the shuffle we all had unfamiliar boxes. Some of the boxes that were missing belonged to us. Finally, it was all straightened and we started to get ready for our new posting.

Our home in High River was again in a building not planned with the comfort of a family in mind. We had very small living quarters on the main floor with a kitchen almost void of cupboards. Most of the main floor was offices and sleeping quarters for the single officers. We had three large bedrooms upstairs and a bathroom larger than the kitchen. The basement was large and contained the prisoner cells, as well as washing and storage areas. I am sure there were fifty steps from the basement to the top floor with the floors and stairs being hardwood, I knew at the first glimpse that my work was cut out for me here.

People that I have talked to considered High River to be one of the friendliest towns in Alberta and I do believe it is so. There was much early history that we found so interesting. We looked forward to raising our family in that quiet area.

Years ago High River got it's name from the Blackfoot Indians. They called it "Ispitsi" meaning High and later, it was called Fort Spitzee. Since it was on the Highwood River, the town became known as High River.

It was the home of the Prince of Wales Ranch, a ranch situated in beautiful country, in the foothills of the Rockies. High River was also the home of many interesting people. Some of the names I still recall. They are Guy Wedick, who started the Calgary stampede and had a ranch in the area, the Cartwright family, and Billy Henry. Others included Bill Holmes, who was the first white child born in the area; Bert Sheppard, and W.O. Mitchell, (well known author and writer). There was also Bill Paul, co-host of the T.V. show "Market Place," country singers Keith Hitchner and Jimmy Lee Hitchner, and Bob Edwards who printed the "Eye Opener." Later purchased by Charles Clark Sr. the grandfather of our former Prime Minister, Honourable Joe Clark, in 1979. There were so many names and stories of that interesting town and we were happy to be a part of it.

Tommy, now a sergeant, was in charge of the detachment. There were several young constables, and a dog trainer who worked with a dog by the name of "King." King was a beautiful, well trained black German Shepherd. He served the southern part of the province, searching for lost persons and property, or life saving in water accidents. Then, of course, there was still Chubby. He still loved to go with any of the men in uniform but had no interest in them if they were in civilian clothes. The second year we were in High River, there was a series of dog poisonings and unfortunately Chubby was one of the victims. We were a very sad family the day we lost him. We decided not to go through that again so, no more dogs.

The schools and teaching staff were some of the finest we could have found any place. Our family grew and became a part of the thriving community.

One special occasion was dear to us regarding a music teacher, Mr. Pickersgill. He came from Ireland and taught music. He taught not only in High River but in the surrounding towns and often made the trip on foot as he didn't have a car. He also had two or three bands that he conducted as well.

One day over a cup of coffee, some of the junior band members' mothers decided that Jack Pickersgill should have a car. Somehow I ended up chairing the drive. We had such wonderful co-operation from not only High River, but the surrounding towns of Blackie, Okotoks, and Nanton. Within three months we had raised sufficient funds to present Mr. Pickersgill with a car. As well we had enough money for the required license, insurance and some left over to go toward a holiday. That was just a little idea of the kind of people we were living among.

One day we returned home from a short outing to find our son had rescued a spotted puppy from out of a near by culvert. It was such a cute wee Heinz 57 variety. The children were so excited that we didn't have the heart to say no to the new addition to the family.

Children and animals belong together, and they had such fun with

Mr. Pickersgill Sr. in High River

Spotty. He hated to see them go to school which was within sight of the house. He had to be restrained on a rope on the clothesline. That little dog persisted in barking until he no longer saw them. He would start again in the afternoon when the children came home after school. It just wasn't a happy situation. When the mounties were on night duty, they would try to get some sleep and it certainly wasn't fair to them. We felt sorry for the children but Spotty had to find a new home so once again we were without a pet.

One pet who lived with us for a short time arrived one day. Tommy brought home a little Spitz dog to cheer up Connie who was ill with some childhood disease. Spitz, was a little ball of white fluff but didn't last long. Although he was loved very much he died of distemper, in spite of our vet's efforts to save him.

Spring arrived, and on May twenty-fourth our children requested to buy firecrackers. We had a little family pow-wow and decided if we all saved $10.00 each, we could buy a little purebred black Chihuahua puppy. That was a popular idea and the children named the puppy Sparkle after the firecrackers they didn't get. Sparkle was such a joy for many years, a loveable well trained dog. As a small puppy she had her photograph taken with the black German Shepherd police dog, King. The way

Connie, Betty and Ron with Spitz pup — Perky, in High River

Police dog, King (stationed in High River with dog master Tom Hograth) and little Chihuahua puppy. Caption in paper was "Wondering if he could be an undercover dog"

111

Sparkle looked up at King gave the idea of the caption in the paper. It said, "The little dog belonging to the Paull family, was looking at King to see if she could be an Undercover Dog."

Sparkle was a great family pet and was the mother of several little full bred Chihuahua puppies. It was an interesting, profitable and educational experience for our town children to see their arrival. They helped in the care of the puppies until they were placed in new homes. All our pets have a special spot in our memories. Even Spotty who lost his home because of his noisy devotion to his little charges.

Sparkle with four puppies in mugs

LIVING IN HARMONY

Living in a detachment that not only housed the officer in charge and his family but several single mounties as well, caused a lot of give and take on all sides.

We tried to teach the children respect for the R.C.M.P. members often causing much questioning when they called them Constable so and so, while their pals called them by their first names. However, their actions were noticed and commended by the officers. Respect for firearms was of major importance. As well, not talking outside the home of anything they might have heard in relationship to anything involving police business. On more than one occasion a teacher mentioned how close mouthed they were. Often different stories cropped up by students regarding something that had happened in the area, but there was never a word spoken from our family who possibly knew more about the happening than any of them. I really think that these were very happy days, and I don't think that the harmony was interrupted.

We really tried to make sure that the single mounties felt free to be with us on any special occasions. Such as birthdays, Christmas, New Years, or any other occasion.

This was the case when one of the mounties contacted measles. There wasn't any place for him to go for the few days he was confined. Our children had already had the measles so we took the mountie into our home and cared for him there. Of course, he was the source of good natured jokes. We laughed with him when he received a bottle of spot remover with a note. It read, "Roses are red, violets are blue, Little spots all over you."

The officer was recovering nicely. About the time he should have been feeling better he broke out with what the doctor diagnosed as chicken pox. That was indeed a very miserable time for him but fortunately for us again it was something our children had already had. Once again the little bottle of spot remover arrived. There was a note that read, "Itchy and bit bitchy too, again you have spots all over you." I doubt if the poor chap thought it was so funny but we were glad that it wasn't a severe attack. It was a happy day for all when he was able to return to duty.

Our kitchen and living room were poorly planned but comfortable. The small kitchen which also acted as the dining room had an archway between, cutting down the area even more. The living room had a door in every corner. Tommy had on several occasions submitted a plan that could change it to make it more liveable. He even offered to do some of the work himself. However, the change never seemed necessary to those in authority.

One day we extended an invitation to the visiting inspector to have lunch with us. In our crowded dining room we gave him what we thought to be the most comfortable place at the table. I guess we had become accustomed to it, but never noticed the many telephone calls our teenagers had at meal time. I suppose that day wasn't unlike others. It was rather embarrassing as each time one of the children excused themselves to answer the phone our poor guest had to get up to let them by. He would have to get up again as they returned to their place at the table. After several such interruptions, the inspector turned to my husband and suggested he resubmit the plans for the change.

Winter in High River. Betty, Connie and Ron

He promised that he would personally recommend them. This was great news to us.

Several changes were made; the rooms remained small but more comfortable. The archway and large chimney were removed, changes were made to the doorways, and cupboards were built. After the entire area was completed, it looked great and what an improvement. We all enjoyed it for the balance of our stay in the detachment building in High River.

On our daughter Betty's thirteenth birthday, an incident happened that one never wants to happen in their area. While we were having a birthday party for Betty in the house, a call came in for the police. Tommy talked to a member of a family who was extremely upset over the drunken behaviour of the man of the house. I guess there was a tussle to get him into the car to bring him to the cell in the detachment house. The mounties removed anything that might be a danger to him and placed him in the detention cell to sleep it off.

Before long he became violent, noisy, and his foul language could be heard upstairs where the young people were present for the birthday party. Tommy decided to take him to the cell in the old town hall and place him under the care of a guard. As he seemed to be much quieter and amiable, Tommy put the drunk fellow in the cell. Rather than embarrass him, the officers didn't remove his belt which held up his loose fitting trousers. As soon as the guard arrived on duty, Tommy returned home.

Paull family in front of home and detachment in High River

I understand that during the evening the guard took a real tongue lashing for disturbing him every time he made a check. The guard finally decided to leave him alone and let him sober up.

Before midnight the dreaded call came that the guard had found that the prisoner had hung himself with his belt. The incident was followed by black anxious days of investigations and visits from a coroner's jury.

The family knew that the local man had suicidal tendencies, but unfortunately the police were not informed of this information. During the inquest, the police were asked why they hadn't taken away the prisoner's belt. When the court questioned Tommy, he mentioned that a man in overalls doesn't have them removed. Even if the overalls have braces attached to them. Tommy also mentioned that, thirteen years to the day, when our eldest daughter was born in the north country, a man had hung himself with his shirt although he had a tie and a belt.

As so often happens at a time like this there were various rumours going around. They ranged from the prisoner being killed in the shuffle when the mounties put him in the cell, to neglect on the part of the police. It wasn't a very happy time for any of us during those days of investigation.

A coroner's jury exonerated the police of all responsibility in the death of that man, even though it was still a trying experience. One we hope would never occur again.

Only on a couple of occasions while in High River was I called on to act as Matron. I was never asked to make a trip out of the home.

One occasion was with a young girl who was travelling with a man with whom she had hitched a ride. She had apparently given him a story about trying to get from the Yukon to her home in the United States. She had a real southern drawl to go with her story. She was an actress. Actually, she was a little runaway from her home in the Yukon and had gone as far as High River. Her only possession was a baby chick that she had acquired along the way. Once again I had been taken in. The sweet little girl that I had taken her for was being returned to her home leaving nothing behind but the baby chick.

I guess progress has been great in many fields but, in those years it was helpful to have a telephone office with cheerful willing operators. If a call came into the office for an officer and they were not in, all I had to do was call the operator at the telephone office. Immediately, a red light was turned on, which was mounted high enough to be seen for miles around the town. Usually within minutes a call was made about the problem and required help was soon on its way. It was always comforting to know that contact was made easily and quickly in those days long before there was two way radio communication.

The radio broadcasts were still needing to be monitored. When the officers were out I tried to take them and answer any calls at the door or on the phone.

Usually, monthly inspections were made by officers. Inspections of not only the office and men's quarters but also of the family dwelling. We were always glad to hear by the grapevine when the inspector was coming. Immediately, cleaning and polishing was the order of the day. Often, the officer would be invited to stay for a meal or afternoon tea, whatever time would allow. Really if we could have relaxed more, I am sure we would have enjoyed these experiences. I think the wives thought the difference between a good report and a poor report depended on the living quarters. Everyone including the children were on their best behaviour. We all would bid good-bye with a sigh of relief when the day was over.

RETIREMENT

Tommy had served for nearly twenty-five years and the time was approaching for retirement. We decided that High River was a good place to stay to see our family of three through high school.

We bought a lot across from the old golf course and near the newly built school. With the years of low wages and the high medical bills, corners had to be cut when it came time to build our house. The plan that we dreamed of was drawn on the back of a calender. From these dreams our house started to become a reality. The basement dug was proof of this reality. We decided that the basement should be made of cement blocks. As a family we bought the cement blocks that were previously used for the plank seats for a five car bingo. We then hauled them to the new lot, the sight of our new home.

Fortunately, Tommy had building experience since his father was a finishing carpenter, and Tommy had helped to build houses before joining the Mounted Police Force. That winter was one of the coldest winters ever. As a family we worked on the house during the annual two week holidays, weekends, and off hours. Finally with the added help of family and friends our house was ready when the retirement day arrived. This was the shortest and easiest move of all. We didn't have the police van to "move it yourself" type move like times before. We had a big moving van that moved us three blocks from the detachment house to our new home. New homes soon started up around us and the choice of where to build our home proved to be a happy one.

High River was a great place, not only for schooling but for other youth activities. As our young people grew up they were active in cubs, scouts and air cadets for boys. Guides, and C.G.I.T for girls. When they were in their teen years they attended one of the finest teen town groups in the province, guided by their leaders, parents and mounties. Once a year, the teenagers put on a formal evening of lunch and dance

Betty, Ron and Connie in front of home in High River

Connie on horseback in front of the home that we built in High River

for the adults of the town and district, held in the community center. This was followed some months later by a formal evening sponsored by the parents and business people for the young people. These were memorable evenings for the teens and the adults. We would all dress up in our finest and we enjoyed great friendships together. These dances always began with the "Grand March." In these events were also parent and teen dance competitions. Tommy and his eldest daughter, Betty won one of these competitions.

There was also a skating rink in the center of town. We felt so fortunate to live in such an active community.

After many years of Tommy working at various occupations, we moved from Alberta to British

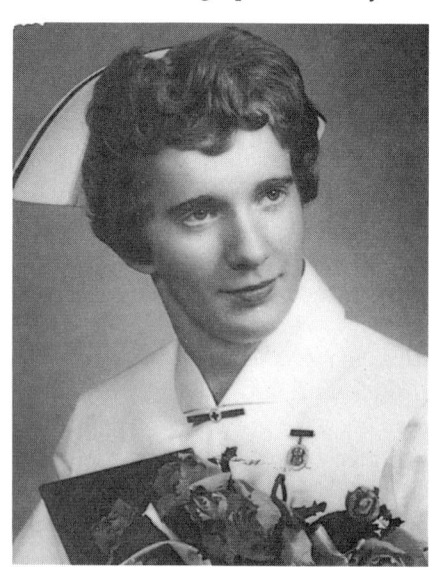

Betty R.N., 1960

Columbia. After several years of living in Richmond, we have now retired in White Rock. Now we have time to reminisce. We look at our three young people who graduated from high school in High River.

Our eldest daughter Betty, an R.N. graduated from nursing training from the Archer Memorial Hospital in Lamont, Alberta as a Registered Nurse. She has nursed for over thirty years in Alberta.

Our youngest daughter, Connie followed a business career and graduated from Mount Royal College in Calgary. Connie's various capabilities have been felt in many areas and she has touched and enhanced many lives.

Both girls married while we were in High River and continue to live and raise their families in Alberta.

Our son Ron followed in his father's footsteps. After his training in the R.C.M.P. in Regina, he was posted in British Columbia, North West Territories, and Yukon. Then back to British Columbia where he has made his home with his family. After a colourful career as Sergeant, he completed 25 years of service.

We have been blessed with nine grandchildren, six girls and three boys.

It was a great experience to be a police officer's wife. We made many wonderful friends, and maybe a few enemies, but had a wealth of experience. I have jotted down some of my recollections. With grateful thanks to so many who helped me along the way I often think about the poem written as guide for us by Major Bagley's wife, the wife of a Royal North West Mounted Police officer. I would like to repeat it here at the end of our story.

Constable Ron R.C.M.P., 1961

Regina 1961. Constable Tommy Paull retired and Constable Ron Paull in training

Two lovely flowers grew side by side,
One was love the other his bride.
When along came a wind on mischief bent
Into their hearts sent a rent.
They fell a fighting and both fell dead
Just from the words that should never have been said.
Two lovely flowers in the garden grew,
Suppose one was Tom and the other one you.
And along came a wind and its merry dance,
It didn't get us, we didn't give it a chance.

Ron (left in front) in Regina at flag raising ceremonies, 1961

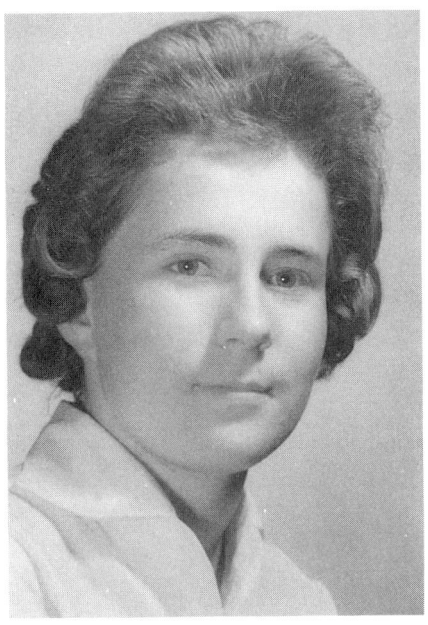

Connie Business grad, 1966

WO 2 Ron Paull of No. 187 air cadet squadron — High River when he received a flying scholarship — July 26, 1958

Tommy and Dorothy just before Tommy retired in 1955

High River. Sergeant Tommy Paull retires

Our 55th wedding anniversary, celebrated with our family. Left to right: Son-in-law Stuart, daughter Betty, Tommy, Dorothy, daughter Connie, son-in-law Alan, daughter-in-law Marilyn, son Ron. Dec. 1992.

March 1993, Delburne, Alberta

Dear Readers,

Scarlet Fever started as some memories of a Banff beginning, for the families future generations. It didn't take me long to realize that this was a history that needed to be shared. As we worked on the manuscript, it became very clear that a visit to Banff would be helpful. A visit would help to set the tone for the entire work.

I had the wonderful opportunity to visit Banff with Mrs. Paull, and her two daughters, Betty and Connie. We were guided through the pages of history of this fascinating place by Mrs. Paull. The mountains are like her best friends. As she introduced each one, she told us their names, and the memories that made each special to her.

The love of God is very evident in both Mr. and Mrs. Paull's lives, and as they told their stories this love shone through. God's love was especially clear when we were in amongst the majestic Rocky Mountains.

I am very pleased to be able to be a part of this work. This way we can share a section of Alberta's history, told through two very special peoples' eyes. A history that might otherwise be lost in the memories of those who lived it.

Yours truly,
Laural Chvojka, editor

Dorothy Paull with daughter Betty in the background in Banff